THIS BOOK BELONGS TO

....

....

PROFESSOR ASTRO CAT'S
FRONTIERS OF
SPACE

WRITTEN BY DR DOMINIC WALLIMAN
DESIGNED AND ILLUSTRATED BY BEN NEWMAN

FLYING EYE BOOKS
LONDON – NEW YORK

Every night, as the Sun sets beyond the horizon, the last rays
of sunlight throw the sky into a beautiful display of colours. As night
approaches, these colours give way to a deep, dark sky covered in a tapestry
of 'little' twinkling stars. When you look up at these stars, and the darkness
in between, you are looking at the biggest thing that exists: the Universe!

But where does our Sun go at night? What are the stars made of and
where did they come from? Are we alone in the Universe or could there
be another boy or girl somewhere on a distant planet looking up at
the sky and wondering these very same ideas?

Our Universe is very complicated, and many scientists spend their
entire lives trying to unravel its greatest secrets – in fact, many of these
secrets are yet to be uncovered. But don't worry, Professor Astro is here to
help, and I am just about the cleverest alley cat you'll ever meet! So batten
down the hatches and buckle up, it's time to blast off and discover
Professor Astro Cat's Frontiers of Space!

THE UNIVERSE

One thing we know for certain about the Universe is that it is really, really big, because it holds all the stars in the sky and much, much more! In fact, the Universe is so big, we are not even sure if it ever ends. Imagine setting off from Earth in a spaceship and travelling forever without hitting anything – that's how big the Universe is. But hold on, let's start at the beginning. First of all, how was the Universe born?

The Universe exploded into existence 13.8 billion years ago in an event called the 'Big Bang'. Everything in the Universe was created in that moment, all the stuff that makes the stars and planets and the energy that flows between them; even space and time were created at the Big Bang. No one really knows why it happened, and to this day it remains one of the great mysteries of science!

The start is the Big Bang:
13.8 billion years ago (13,799,000,000 years).

377 thousand years (377,000 years) after the Big Bang:
Atoms form and photons of light travel freely.

Through time, the Universe spread out in all directions and began to take shape. From the swirling energy, tiny particles popped into existence. After a few hundred thousand years, they collected together into atoms, the basic building blocks of everything we can see in the Universe. Also at this time, light was released and free to fly through the Universe. Wowee!

It wasn't until hundreds of millions of years later that the atoms collected together into great clouds, from which the first generation of stars was born. These stars collected together into galaxies, and the Universe started to become the one that we see in the sky at night today. The Universe is still expanding now and will carry on getting bigger and bigger forever!

500 million years (500,000,000 years) after the Big Bang: The first galaxies form.

200 million years (200,000,000 years) after the Big Bang: The first stars form.

Fact: You can hear the echo of the Big Bang yourself! Just listen to a detuned radio: one crackle in a hundred is made by leftover light from the Big Bang, stretched over billions of years into radio waves.

ZZZZZZt

KKKKKt

ZZZZZZt

KKKKKt

CRACKLE

KKKKKt

ZZZZZZt

THE BIRTH OF A STAR

You may think that the only time you can see stars is at night, but you'd be wrong – our Sun is actually a star and you see it every day! The Sun is quite an ordinary star and has kept a stable temperature and brightness since there has been life on Earth. All the other stars are much further away than our Sun, which is why they look so small in the night sky, but they all have their own extraordinary stories to tell. So, how did they begin?

The stars formed out of clouds of hydrogen gas, which were left over either from the Big Bang or from earlier exploded stars.

Over time, gravity pulled this gas together into clumps, where it started to spin and heat up.

This continued until the gas was dense and hot enough to combine and then, in a flash of light, a new star was born.

That is just incredible!

WOAH!

TYPES OF STARS

Giant stars are very large, which means they are extremely hot and bright. Sadly, this incredible power causes them to burn their fuel very quickly, so they have a shorter lifespan than our Sun.

GIANT STAR

RED DWARF STAR

Red dwarf stars are smaller than our Sun, but live for an incredibly long time. They are so small that they have a relatively slow and stable nuclear reaction at their cores that will last for hundreds of billions of years.

Brown dwarf stars are the smallest stars in the Universe. They are not big enough to fuse hydrogen together, but can be big enough to create other elements. Brown dwarfs are very small and don't give off much light, so they are very difficult to discover.

BROWN DWARF STAR

MAIN SEQUENCE STAR

Our Sun is known as a 'main sequence' star, and there are many others like it. Main sequence stars make up 90% of the stars we can see and are the most likely to have planets that support life.

They are so beautiful!

Amazing!

GALAXIES

All of the stars we see from Earth are part of a big group of stars called a galaxy! Galaxies are made up of vast swarms of stars, swirling around like a giant space whirlpool. Our galaxy is called the Milky Way and looks a bit like a Catherine wheel firework. It contains more stars than anyone could count in a lifetime and is constantly spinning very, very slowly – so slowly, in fact, that it takes 225 million years to complete a full cycle.

You can see the Milky Way in the night sky with your own eyes if you go far into the countryside, away from the city lights. It forms a milky band of light stretching across the sky, and is quite a beautiful thing to see.

Outside the Milky Way are lots of other galaxies, all made of countless numbers of stars. These galaxies come in all shapes and sizes, some swirling around like our own and others are big disordered balls of stars that look like giant swarms of bees. You can see a couple of galaxies with your eyes, but most of them are so far away that you need a big telescope to spot them. There are galaxies stretching away into the depths of space as far as our most powerful telescopes can see, and there are certainly even more beyond that.

The closest spiral galaxy to the Milky Way is the Andromeda galaxy, around 2.5 million light years away. It is so far away that the light we see from it has been travelling through space for 2.5 million years. This means that we see the Andromeda galaxy as it was in the ancient past, before humans even existed on Earth!

The further you look into space, the further you are looking into the past, so the furthest galaxy we have discovered is very, very old. It is called UDFj-39546284 and because it is at the very edge of the visible Universe, we see it as it was not long after the Big Bang.

THE SPEED OF LIGHT

Because things in space are so far away, we don't measure distances in miles or kilometres, but in light years! One light year is the distance that light travels in one Earth year. Light is the fastest thing in the Universe, and it can cover mind-boggling distances in a short space of time – it is so fast that it could travel all the way around the Earth 7½ times in a second!

THE SUN

The Sun is the most important star in our sky, giving light and heat to us and all living things on Earth. It is just like all the other stars in the sky, although it looks much bigger. It is so big that if the Sun was hollow it would take a million Earths to fill it up. Just like all stars, the Sun is a giant fireball – an explosion that just kept on going.

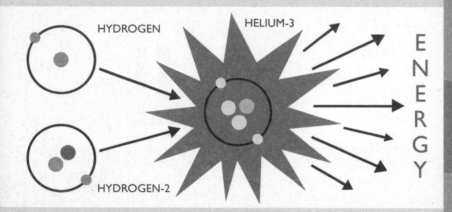

HYDROGEN
HELIUM-3
HYDROGEN-2
ENERGY

The light and heat given off by the Sun comes from a process called a fusion reaction. The great pressure and temperature at the centre of the Sun makes atoms stick together and releases lots of energy. The Sun is made of super-hot gases, 74% hydrogen, 25% helium and 1% other elements. You might have heard of helium before, as it is what people put in balloons to make them float in the air. You could use hydrogen to do the same thing, but people avoid it because it can easily explode!

Did you know?
The sunlight we experience on Earth takes 8 minutes and 20 seconds to get to us from the surface of the Sun, but 30,000 years to get from the centre of the Sun to its surface.

CORONA
The hottest part of the Sun happens outside in the corona, where temperatures can reach up to 20 million degrees Celsius (36,000,032 degrees Fahrenheit) in solar flares! That is even hotter than the fusion reaction in the centre of the Sun! Although the corona is normally about 2 million degrees Celsius (36 million degrees Fahrenheit).

The Sun is really, really hot: 5,500 degrees Celsius (9,932 degrees Fahrenheit) on the surface and a massive 15 million degrees Celsius (27,000,032 degrees Fahrenheit) in the centre.

CONVECTIVE ZONE

RADIATIVE ZONE

THE CORE

PHOTOSPHERE

CHROMOSPHERE

The chromosphere is the coolest part of the Sun at around 4,300 degrees Celsius (7,772 degrees Fahrenheit), although this is still hot enough to melt a spaceship.

The Sun occasionally gets sunspots. These are cooler areas of the surface and are caused by the Sun's magnetism. The Sun releases lots of particles and radiation around sunspots in solar flares.

Although we see the Sun move across the sky every day, this is just an illusion. Really, the Sun stays in the same place and the Earth is spinning round and round. The Earth makes one full spin every day, and this is what makes the Sun rise and set – just like if you spin around next to a bright lamp, it looks like the lamp is flying around you.

SOLAR FLARE

As well as giving off light and heat, the Sun fires off loads of tiny particles which make the solar wind. We are protected from most of these particles by the Earth's magnetic field, which acts as an invisible force field, bending them away. We can see beautiful lights in the sky at the poles when lots of particles hit the magnetosphere – these are called the Aurora Borealis, or the Northern Lights; or Aurora Australis, the Southern Lights.

SOLAR WINDS

EARTH'S MAGNETIC FIELD

THE SOLAR SYSTEM

Our solar system has eight planets in it, which all orbit around the Sun in the same direction. The Sun is the centre of the solar system, and because it is so big it has a huge amount of gravity which holds all of the planets together and keeps them moving around the Sun in massive circles called orbits. Gravity is a force that acts like an invisible rope between the Sun and all the planets, and it stops them from flying off into space.

The first four planets out from the Sun are all made of rock and metal, and these are called terrestrial planets. They have solid surfaces that you could walk about on and are all situated close to the Sun.

The last four planets are all made of gas, which means that if you tried to stand on the surface you would fall straight through. These four 'gas giants' are much, much bigger than the terrestrial planets and are all very far away from each other.

For a long time, it was thought that the furthest planet away in our solar system was Pluto, which is a dwarf planet that lies beyond Neptune in an area called the Kuiper belt. Recently, scientists decided that it was no longer a planet, because there are other objects in the Kuiper belt that are the same size or bigger than Pluto – like Eris, a planetoid discovered in 2005. There are thousands of other Kuiper belt objects, all made of rock and ice.

Sorry, Pluto, but you are no longer considered a planet!

PLUTO

MERCURY

THE SUN

VENUS

EARTH

MARS

ASTEROID BELT

In between Mars and Jupiter is the asteroid belt. Asteroids are similar to planets, made of rock and metals, but are much smaller. Billions of years ago, before the planets formed, the whole solar system looked like a big asteroid belt, but over time these asteroids collected together to form the planets. Astronomers think that Jupiter's massive gravity kept the asteroids in the asteroid belt apart and stopped them from collecting together. In this case, the asteroid belt is the planet that never was.

JUPITER

If the Earth was a cherry tomato, what size would all the other planets be?
Of course, they wouldn't be this close to each other. But if the Earth was a cherry tomato in your hand, the Sun would be 500 metres away and 4 metres wide.

MERCURY
Peppercorn

VENUS
Cherry

MARS
Pea

EARTH
Cherry
tomato

JUPITER
Watermelon

SATURN
Large
grapefruit

URANUS
Apple

NEPTUNE
Lime

URANUS

PLUTO

ERIS

SATURN

NEPTUNE

KUIPER BELT

EARTH

Our home in the Universe is a blue and green ball of rock called the Earth. The Earth holds all of the life that has ever been discovered, and what a fantastic and beautiful variety of life it is!

There is a good reason why the Earth has so many different plants and animals on it, and that is because the conditions are just right for life to exist. Just like Goldilocks, who didn't like her porridge too hot or too cold, plants and animals don't like their planet to be too hot or too cold. The Earth is at just the right distance from the Sun so that the temperature is just right for life to flourish.

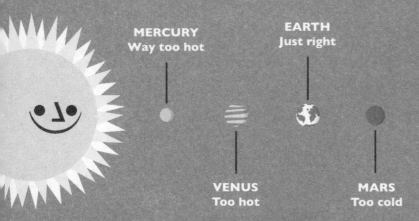

MERCURY Way too hot

EARTH Just right

VENUS Too hot

MARS Too cold

We have the only planet in the solar system that has lots of liquid water, a very important part of life. If we were too close to the Sun, all of the water would dry up and it would be like living in a desert. If we were too far away from the Sun, all of the water would freeze and it would be like living at the North Pole. The Earth is in just the right place for liquid water: the Goldilocks zone!

The layer of air that surrounds the Earth is called the atmosphere, and it is like a warm blanket around the Earth, protecting us from space. Although the Sun gives life through its heat and light, the Sun's rays can also be harmful. That is why we put on sunscreen in the summer, to stop us from getting burned. The atmosphere protects us from most of the harmful rays of the Sun, and also keeps the heat of the Earth in, stopping it from getting too cold.

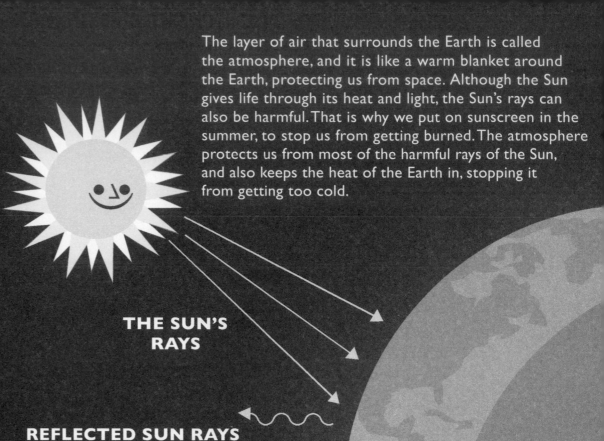

THE SUN'S RAYS

REFLECTED SUN RAYS FROM THE EARTH'S SURFACE

We humans have to be careful about what we put into the atmosphere. In the last few years, the gases people have released from power plants, cars and deforestation have made the atmosphere thicker – and just like a thicker blanket, this is causing the planet to warm up. This global warming melts our ice caps and raises our sea levels. This is bad for us and the Earth!

The Earth flies through space around the Sun at an incredible speed: 1,000 miles every minute (or about 1,500 kilometres every minute). Even at this speed, it takes a whole year for the Earth to go all the way around the Sun.

The seasons are caused by the Earth having a tilted axis. Instead of spinning around straight up, like a spinning top, it leans over a little bit. When we are tilted towards the Sun, it flies high in the sky and we have long days and everything is lovely and warm: the summer. When we are tilted away from the Sun, it is low in the sky and we have short, cold days: the winter.

This picture is for the Northern hemisphere. The seasons are the opposite way around for the Southern hemisphere; Christmas is in the summer in Australia.

EARTH'S GRAVITY

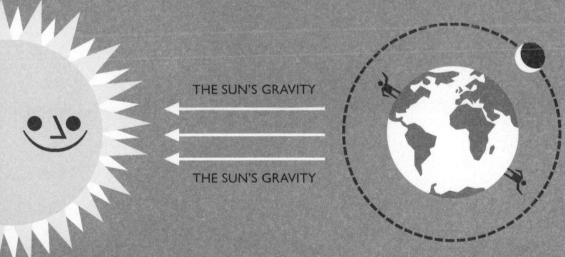

While the Earth is spinning and flying through space, we don't notice any movement. This is because we are kept stuck to the ground by a thing called gravity. Gravity is like an invisible elastic band between us and the Earth, and is what stops us from flying off into space. Even if you jump really high, you will always come back down. Gravity is everywhere!

It is the force that stops the air from wandering off into space, which is just as well, as we need air to breathe. It also keeps the Moon going around the Earth, and the Earth going around the Sun. In fact, everything in the Universe is tied to everything else by the force of gravity.

THE MOON

The Moon is our closest neighbour in space, a massive ball of rock thought to have been formed from a collision between the Earth and another planet billions of years ago. It now floats serenely around the Earth, an ever-present companion in the sky.

Whenever we look at the Moon, we always see the same side staring back at us. This is because the Moon's spin slowed down over time as it used up its energy moving the tides on the Earth – so we never see the far side of the Moon. People always wondered what the other side looked like, which was a mystery until 1959 when a Russian spaceship, Lunar 3, went behind the Moon and took some photos. The far side of the Moon is much rougher and has more craters than the near side.

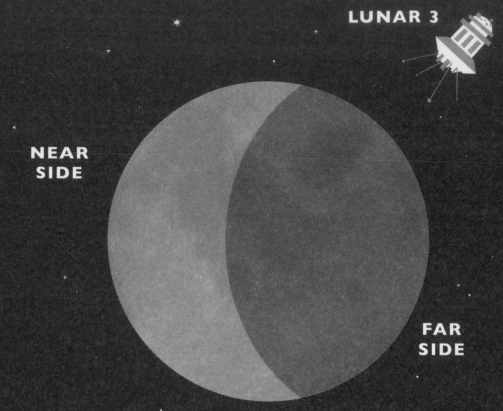

LUNAR 3

NEAR SIDE

FAR SIDE

Is the Moon made of cheese?

The Moon's cratered surface does look a bit like a piece of Swiss cheese! But no, the Moon is made of very much the same thing as we find in rocks on Earth: sand and metals.

It takes the Moon 27½ days to orbit around the Earth, which is around a month for us. The Moon used to be in orbit much closer to the Earth, but scientists have discovered that the Moon has been steadily drifting further away from us by nearly 4 centimetres a year. This distance is so small that it would take many years for us to notice the Moon shrinking in our night sky.

The Moon is much, much smaller than Earth. Do you remember how many Earths could fit in the Sun? Well, it would take 50 of our Moon to fill the Earth. Gosh, that's a lot of Moons!

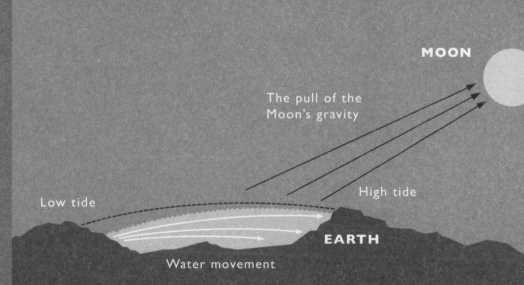

MOON

The pull of the Moon's gravity

High tide

Low tide

EARTH

Water movement

THE MOON AND EARTH'S TIDES

Even though the Moon is far away from us, it has very important effects on the Earth through its gravity. Because of the Moon, the seas and oceans on the Earth bulge out either side. As the Earth spins, it moves through the high and low water regions, causing the water to come in and out at the seaside. The Moon pulls our tide higher and moves it in and out of our shores. If it wasn't for the Moon, we wouldn't have any tides… and starfish would be very confused!

THE MANY FACES OF THE MOON

Throughout the month, the Moon appears to change shape from a crescent to a full moon and back again. This is because the Sun shines on different parts of the Moon at different times of the month. Really, we are seeing the Moon's night-time move over its surface

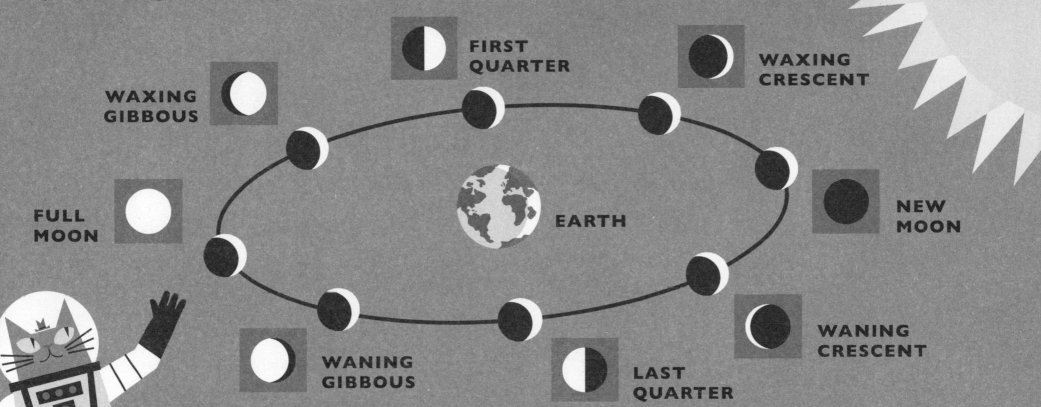

FIRST QUARTER

WAXING CRESCENT

WAXING GIBBOUS

EARTH

NEW MOON

FULL MOON

WANING GIBBOUS

LAST QUARTER

WANING CRESCENT

ECLIPSES

To us on Earth, the Sun and the Moon look the same size in the sky. This is an amazing coincidence, because really they are massively different sizes. The Sun is much, much bigger than the Moon, but also happens to be much, much further away. Sometimes, when the orbits line up just right, the Moon will float in front of the Sun, completely covering it and casting a shadow onto the Earth. This is called a solar eclipse. A lunar eclipse is when the Earth's shadow moves across the Moon. In this case, we would see a bright Moon turn dark red for several hours.

When an eclipse happens, you can be in broad daylight, but as the Moon starts to move across the Sun everything starts to get cold and dark. The Moon completely covers the Sun for up to 7½ minutes before moving on its way and allowing the Sun to burst forth once again. If you ever see an eclipse, you have to remember to avoid looking directly at the Sun – it is so bright, it can damage your eyes.

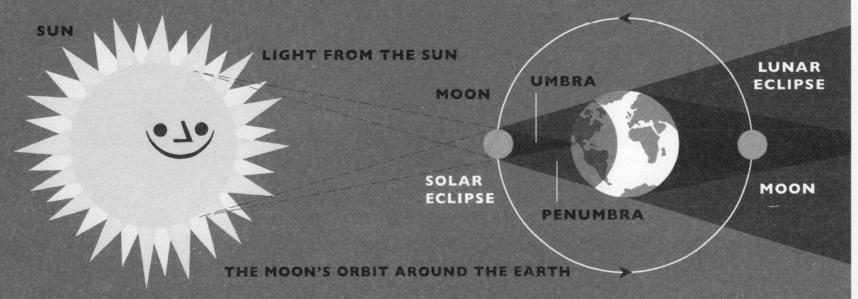

SUN

LIGHT FROM THE SUN

MOON

UMBRA

LUNAR ECLIPSE

SOLAR ECLIPSE

PENUMBRA

MOON

THE MOON'S ORBIT AROUND THE EARTH

Total Eclipse
Moon completely covers Sun.

Annular Eclipse
Moon completely in front of Sun but not full coverage.

Partial Eclipse
Moon covers part of Sun.

SPACE TRAVEL

For years, people wondered what it would be like to fly up above the sky, out of the Earth's atmosphere, and travel into space. The first beings to leave the Earth were not people, but animals. The first animals in space were fruit flies in 1947.

After that, scientists in the USA and Russia tried sending larger animals into space to see if it was possible for humans to travel to the stars. These brave animals gave their lives for science.

The first animal to make a full orbit of the Earth was Laika, a stray dog rescued from the streets of Moscow and rocketed to fame aboard a Soviet spaceship.

My dad went to school with her!

ENTER

LAIKA

ALBERT II

Holy cheeseballs!

The first primate in space was a rhesus monkey called Albert II, launched into space by the US space programme (NASA). This was an important experiment because monkeys and apes are our closest relatives in the animal kingdom, so the scientists learned a lot about what might happen to us if we went into space.

In 1961, this dream became a reality for one man, cosmonaut Yuri Gagarin, who was sent into space on the top of a gigantic Soviet rocket. He flew once all the way around the planet in his tiny spacecraft Vostok 1 and landed safely back in Russia, the first human to travel in space. Since then, many others have followed in his footsteps, travelling into orbit, to space stations and even to the Moon.

Wowee!

YURI GAGARIN

APOLLO 11

JULY 16TH 1969: After years of rigorous physical and academic training, three men – Buzz Aldrin, Neil Armstrong and Michael Collins – launched from the Kennedy Space Center on Merritt Island, Florida, USA. In a capsule at the top of the giant Apollo 11 spacecraft, they were blasted into space at supersonic speeds, prepared for the mission ahead.

JULY 19TH 1969: Three days after the launch from Earth, the Apollo 11 spacecraft arrived at the Moon and fired its retro-rocket to enter lunar orbit.

JULY 20TH 1969: Neil Armstrong and Buzz Aldrin squeezed into the lunar module and were launched towards the surface, leaving Michael Collins in the command module orbiting the Moon. Neil guided the lander down to the surface with Buzz's help. The lander overshot its planned landing spot, but managed to land safely despite being dangerously low on fuel.

JULY 21ST 1969: History was made when Neil Armstrong put his left foot onto the surface of the Moon: the first human to walk on another planetary body. After getting used to the low gravity and slippery moondust, Neil and Buzz explored the surface of the Moon, collecting rock and soil samples. They also planted an American flag, unpacked scientific equipment to measure moonquakes and took lots of photos of the surface.

JULY 22ND 1969: After a night's sleep in the lunar module, the astronauts blasted off from the surface and reconnected with Michael Collins and the command module in orbit.

JULY 24TH 1969: The command module ripped through the Earth's atmosphere in a blaze of heat and splashed upside down in the Pacific Ocean. They were soon the right way up with the help of some flotation devices, and were rescued by helicopter.

Neil Armstrong

Buzz Aldrin

Michael Collins

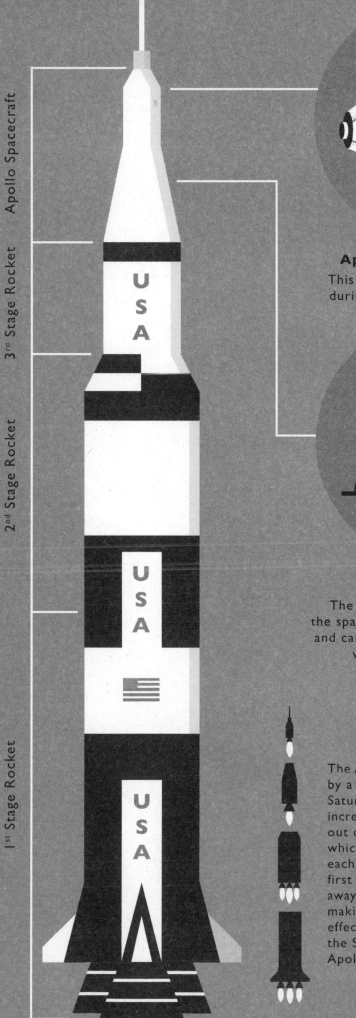

Apollo Spacecraft

3rd Stage Rocket

2nd Stage Rocket

1st Stage Rocket

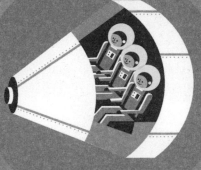

Apollo Command Module

This was where the astronauts sat during their journey to the Moon.

Lunar Module

The lunar module was the part of the spacecraft that landed on the Moon and carried just two of the astronauts, while the third piloted the command module.

Up, Up and Away!

The Apollo spacecraft was launched by a three-stage rocket called the Saturn 5. This rocket needed to be incredibly strong to push the spacecraft out of Earth's gravity and into space, which is why it was split into stages, each working one at a time. When the first tank ran out of fuel, it was thrown away, removing the dead weight and making the next tank of fuel more effective. By doing this three times, the Saturn 5 rocket propelled the Apollo spacecraft to the Moon.

GOING TO THE MOON

The first successful landing on the Moon took place in 1969, and the journey took the Apollo II astronauts 3 days. The following diagram illustrates how they got there and back home safely.

1. 1st stage rocket falls away and 2nd stage rocket is ignited to get into orbit.

2. 2nd stage rocket falls away and 3rd stage rocket is ignited.

3. Spacecraft is released from 3rd stage rocket.

4. Spacecraft turns to face lunar module and release it from storage.

5. Spacecraft connects with lunar module and breaks free from 3rd stage rocket.

The blue line represents the journey from Earth to the Moon. The yellow line represents the journey back from the Moon to the safety of Earth.

EARTH

MOON

In order to gain enough speed to break away from Earth's gravitational pull, the Apollo II rocket had to complete a loop of the Earth. This acted like a slingshot and fired the rocket at an incredible speed towards the Moon.

9. Lunar module reconnects with spacecraft, and astronauts climb aboard command module.

12. Command module gets extremely hot when re-entering Earth's atmosphere.

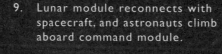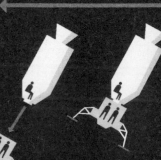

8. Lunar module has its own rockets to leave Moon's surface with.

6. Two astronauts get into lunar module and pilot it down to Moon's surface. One astronaut stays on board to fly spacecraft.

10. Lunar module is left floating empty in space.

11. Command module separates from spacecraft and heads into Earth's orbit.

THE MOON'S SURFACE

13. Once in Earth's atmosphere, command module opens its parachutes to land safely in the ocean.

7. Astronauts explore Moon and collect rock samples to bring back to Earth.

HOW A ROCKET WORKS

Rockets get up into space by burning rocket fuel, which sends gases blasting out of the bottom. Because these gases come out so quickly, it makes the top of the rocket start to move upwards, and the more gases that come out, the faster the rocket flies. It's like riding on the top of a controlled explosion!

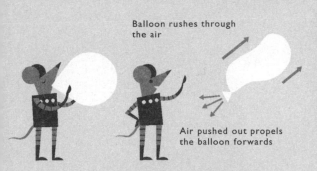

Balloon rushes through the air

Air pushed out propels the balloon forwards

The same thing happens when you let go of a blown-up balloon. The sides of the balloon are constantly trying to push the air inside out of the hole. When you let go, this air comes rushing out and the balloon flies forwards really fast!

In a rocket, it isn't the sides pushing the gas out, it's the engines. They combine rocket fuel with liquid oxygen and set it on fire, which makes it rush out at great speeds. Whoooosh!

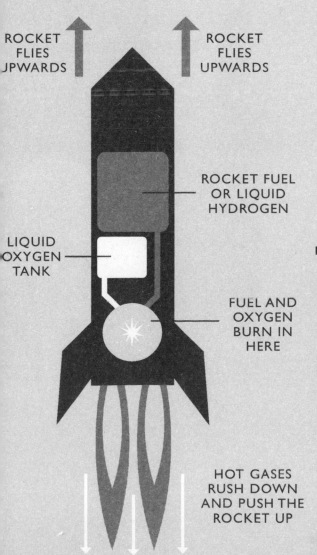

ROCKET FLIES UPWARDS

ROCKET FLIES UPWARDS

ROCKET FUEL OR LIQUID HYDROGEN

LIQUID OXYGEN TANK

FUEL AND OXYGEN BURN IN HERE

HOT GASES RUSH DOWN AND PUSH THE ROCKET UP

Eating food in space is very different to eating food on Earth. When you are in the middle of space, you are completely weightless because there is no gravity to hold you down. This means that all your food and drink just floats about in mid-air, and could make a terrible mess! This can actually be very dangerous in space, because food or liquids could get into important electrical systems and cause short circuits, putting the astronauts in danger.

To dine safely in space, astronauts on the Apollo 11 mission ate their food out of bags using a spoon. Before the mission, all the water was taken out of the food to make it last longer. While on the mission, the astronauts would just add hot water to make their meal.

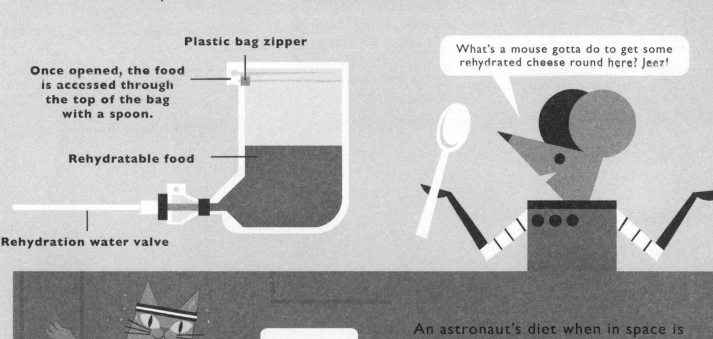

Plastic bag zipper

Once opened, the food is accessed through the top of the bag with a spoon.

Rehydratable food

Rehydration water valve

What's a mouse gotta do to get some rehydrated cheese round here? Jeez!

No pain, no gain!

An astronaut's diet when in space is very important, because the human body starts to get weak in zero gravity. Astronauts have to exercise regularly in space and eat well in order to keep their bones and muscles strong. Plenty of meat and vegetables and a healthy dose of calcium will do the trick! Dehydrated milkshakes, anyone?

THE APOLLO MOON SUIT 1969

Grumman Moon Suit
1963

1960s US Prototype
Capsule Suit

Early NASA Apollo
Pressure Suit

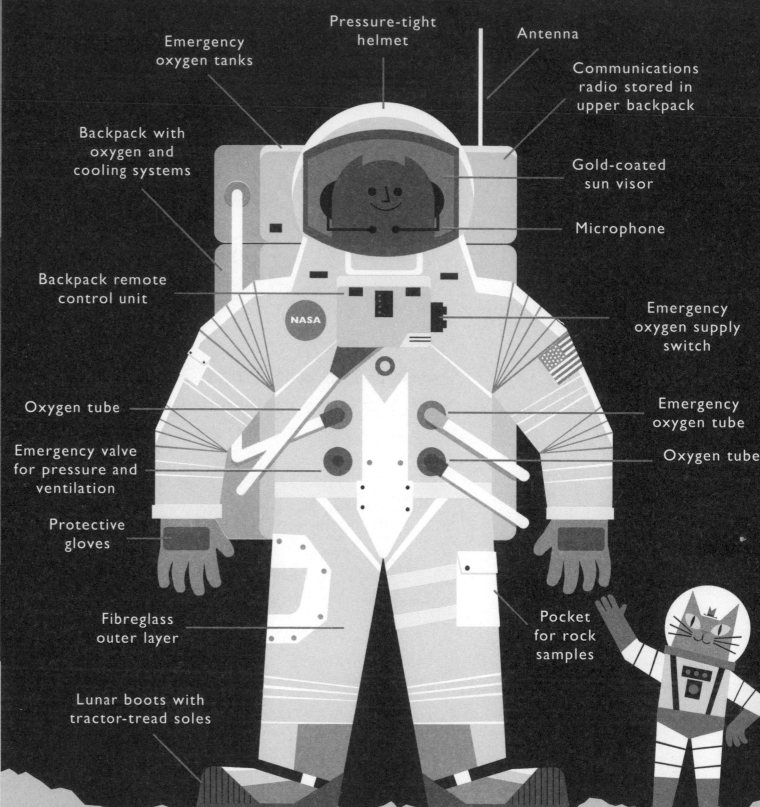

Emergency
oxygen tanks

Pressure-tight
helmet

Antenna

Communications
radio stored in
upper backpack

Backpack with
oxygen and
cooling systems

Gold-coated
sun visor

Microphone

Backpack remote
control unit

Emergency
oxygen supply
switch

Oxygen tube

Emergency
oxygen tube

Emergency valve
for pressure and
ventilation

Oxygen tube

Protective
gloves

Fibreglass
outer layer

Pocket
for rock
samples

Lunar boots with
tractor-tread soles

On July 21st 1969, the astronauts Neil Armstrong and Buzz Aldrin made history by being the first people to walk on the Moon. They wore the Apollo 11 space suits on the surface to protect them from the vacuum of space. The suit contained everything needed to keep the astronauts alive in the hostile environment, including pressurised air and layers of protection from extreme temperatures and radiation. Each space suit was custom-made for each astronaut and could be worn in relative comfort for up to 115 hours. On Earth, the suits were very heavy to wear, but on the Moon they weighed almost nothing at all.

APOLLO LUNAR MODULE

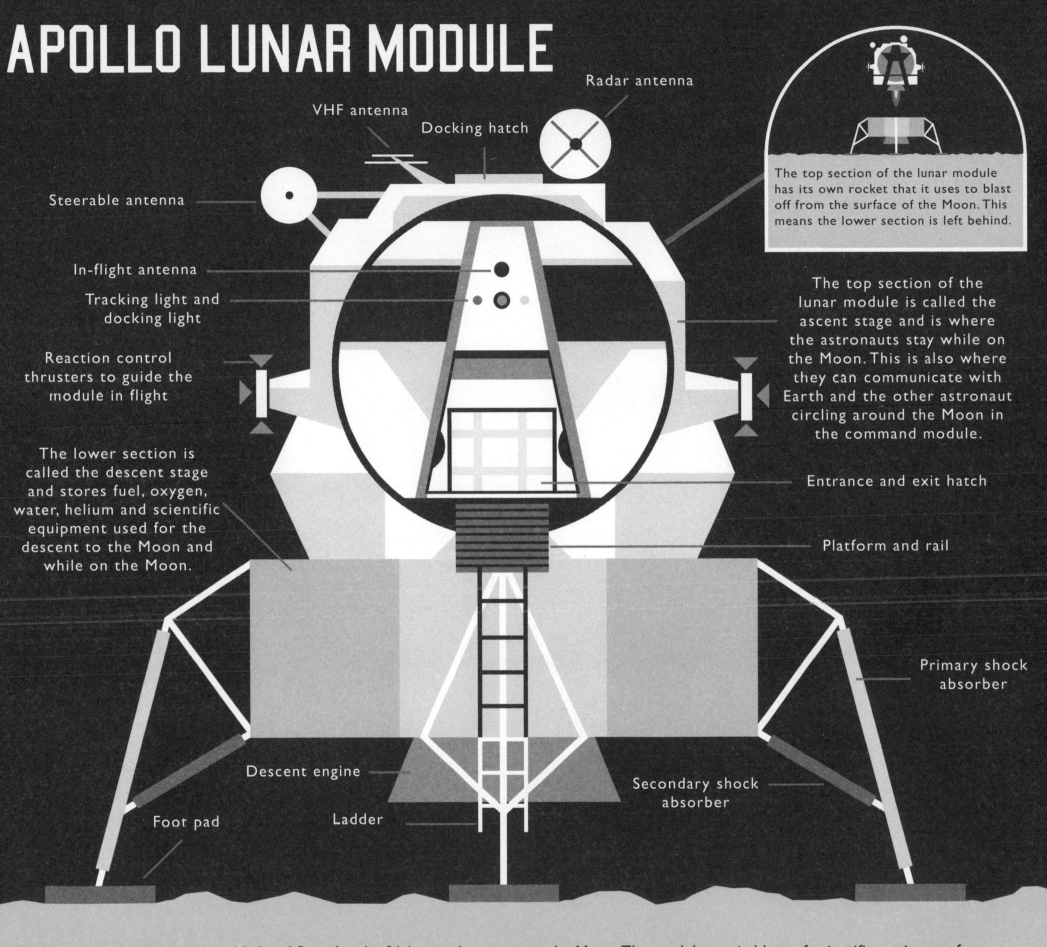

Radar antenna

VHF antenna

Docking hatch

Steerable antenna

In-flight antenna

Tracking light and docking light

Reaction control thrusters to guide the module in flight

The lower section is called the descent stage and stores fuel, oxygen, water, helium and scientific equipment used for the descent to the Moon and while on the Moon.

The top section of the lunar module has its own rocket that it uses to blast off from the surface of the Moon. This means the lower section is left behind.

The top section of the lunar module is called the ascent stage and is where the astronauts stay while on the Moon. This is also where they can communicate with Earth and the other astronaut circling around the Moon in the command module.

Entrance and exit hatch

Platform and rail

Primary shock absorber

Descent engine

Secondary shock absorber

Foot pad

Ladder

The lunar module was home to Neil and Buzz for the 21 hours they were on the Moon. The module carried lots of scientific equipment for them to collect rock samples and make discoveries about the Moon. It was made of two parts: the descent stage, which stayed on the surface, and the ascent stage, which brought the astronauts safely back to the command module. It was really important that the astronauts landed safely on the surface of the Moon. Any mistakes, such as the lander falling over or one of the module's legs breaking, would have stranded the poor astronauts on the Moon, unable to return home. Through a combination of brilliant engineering and the skill of Neil and Buzz, the module was set down safely, letting the astronauts be the first people to explore the surface of the Moon.

You can't breathe on the Moon, because it has no air, so the astronauts needed to carry their own air with them wherever they went. Also, because there is no air on the Moon, it is completely silent.

One side of the Moon always faces away from us on the Earth. It's called the 'dark side of the Moon' because we can't see it from Earth, but this is a bit of a mistake, because when this side faces the Sun it is very bright and hot.

Eek! I'm scared of the dark!

I told you this earlier, Astro Mouse. The Moon is not made of cheese.

I was just double-checking!

The Moon does not have a magnetic field like the Earth, with a North and South Pole, but parts of the surface are weakly magnetic. This means that you couldn't use a compass to navigate the Moon.

There is no wind on the Moon, and so there is no erosion. This means that the footprints left by the astronauts will stay there for millions of years.

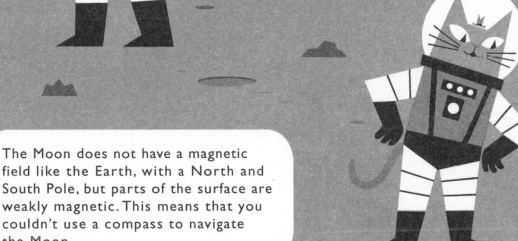

MODERN ROCKETS

The rockets that flew to the Moon could only make one trip and were incredibly expensive to produce. The space shuttle was designed by NASA to be a reusable spaceship which could launch into orbit like a rocket, then fly back down to Earth like an airplane. It was first launched in 1981 and went on a total of 135 missions before being decommissioned in 2011. There were 5 shuttles in total: Atlantis, Challenger, Columbia, Discovery and Endeavour, but only three of them exist today, because Challenger and Columbia were lost in accidents.

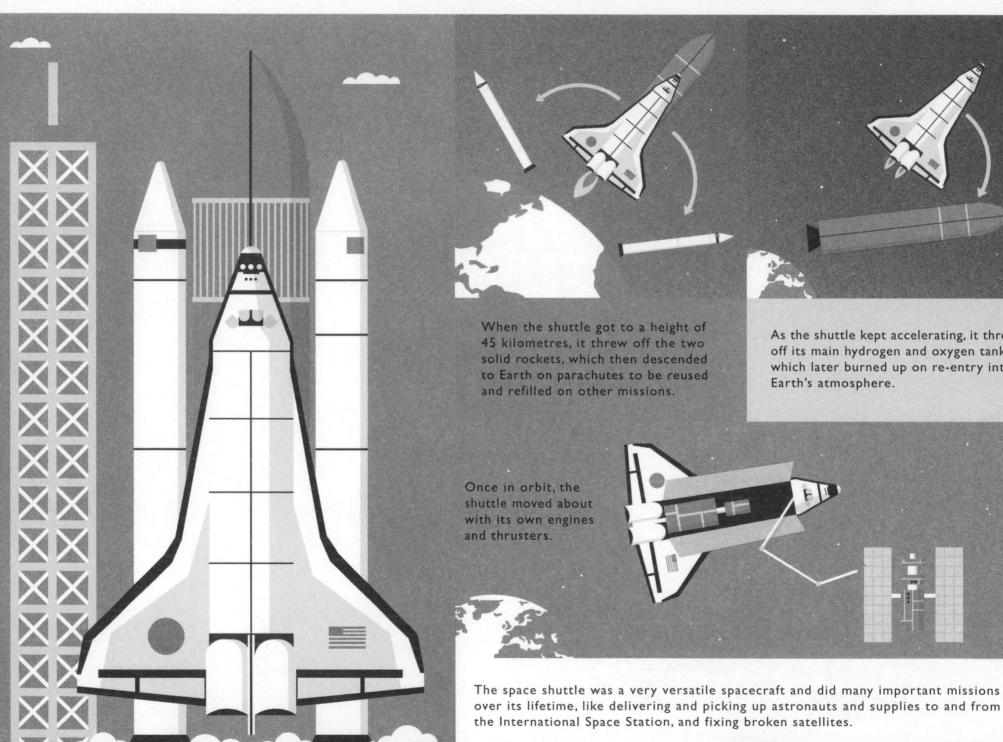

When the shuttle got to a height of 45 kilometres, it threw off the two solid rockets, which then descended to Earth on parachutes to be reused and refilled on other missions.

As the shuttle kept accelerating, it threw off its main hydrogen and oxygen tank, which later burned up on re-entry into Earth's atmosphere.

Once in orbit, the shuttle moved about with its own engines and thrusters.

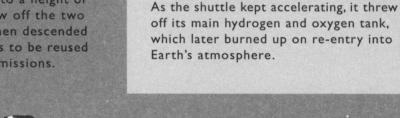

The space shuttle was a very versatile spacecraft and did many important missions over its lifetime, like delivering and picking up astronauts and supplies to and from the International Space Station, and fixing broken satellites.

The shuttle landed on a runway just like an airplane.

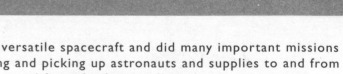

When sitting on the launch pad, the shuttle was attached to two rockets and a large orange tank full of liquid hydrogen and liquid oxygen fuel. The shuttle blasted off the launch pad with its three main engines burning fuel from the main tank, assisted by the solid rockets either side.

MODERN SPACE SUITS

Space suits have changed a lot since the bulky suits that the astronauts wore on the Apollo missions. It is very difficult to make a good space suit, because it needs to be very strong to protect the wearer, but also flexible enough so that they can move about and perform delicate tasks like fixing spaceships. To fight against the emptiness of space, the suits are pumped up with air like a balloon – a bubble of the Earth's atmosphere protecting the astronaut. If the suit didn't have this pressurised air, the astronaut's skin would swell up to about twice the size, making them look like a bodybuilder!

I think I put my space suit on wrong!

Aha... hahahaha!

When on a spacewalk, astronauts also wear a jet pack, which uses nitrogen thrusters to stop them from drifting away into space.

Cameras and communication devices are attached to the top of the jet pack.

An operations manual is attached to their forearm.

The nitrogen thrusters can be found either side of the jet pack.

When an astronaut works in the middle of space, they also need extra protection against ultraviolet rays and radiation from the Sun, as well as layers of material to protect against tiny space rocks, which can reach incredible speeds and pierce a hole in the suit! This would be very bad for our brave astronaut.

INTERNATIONAL SPACE STATION

The International Space Station, or ISS for short, orbits the Earth, zooming through space above our heads at 5 miles per second. About the size of a football field, it was built bit by bit over many years by linking modules together in space. It is used as a science lab where astronauts and cosmonauts perform science experiments and learn what it is like to live in space for long periods of time. Normally there are 3 people on board at any one time, but there can be as many as 10!

The ISS completes 15.7 orbits of the Earth each day.

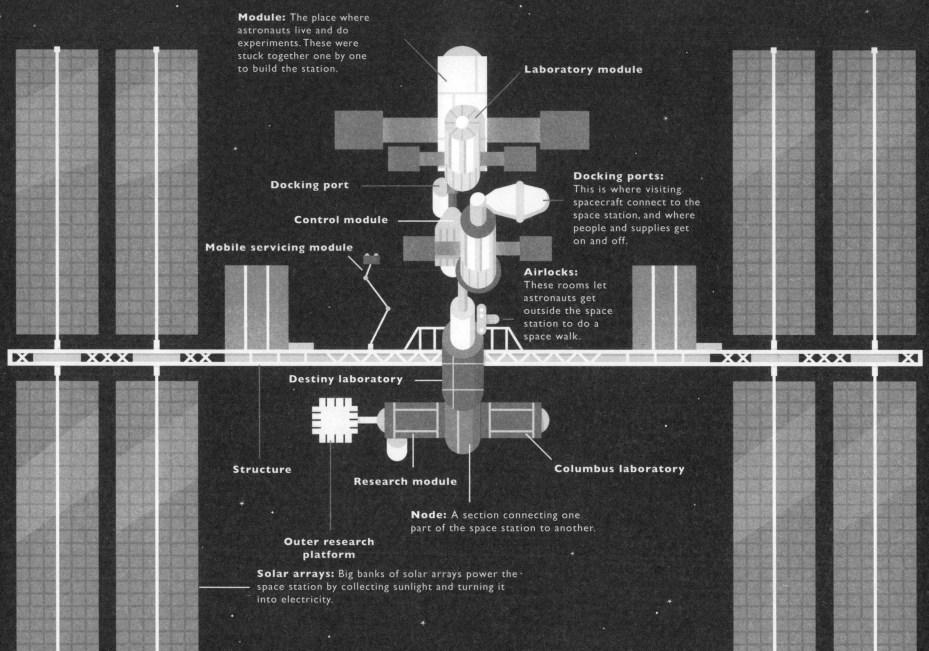

Module: The place where astronauts live and do experiments. These were stuck together one by one to build the station.

Laboratory module

Docking port

Control module

Mobile servicing module

Docking ports: This is where visiting spacecraft connect to the space station, and where people and supplies get on and off.

Airlocks: These rooms let astronauts get outside the space station to do a space walk.

Destiny laboratory

Structure

Research module

Columbus laboratory

Node: A section connecting one part of the space station to another.

Outer research platform

Solar arrays: Big banks of solar arrays power the space station by collecting sunlight and turning it into electricity.

Who built the ISS?

To build the International Space Station, the American, European, Russian, Japanese and Canadian space agencies all came together to make the largest space station ever. Before and after the ISS, there have been other space stations, such as the Russian Mir, which was in operation for 15 years. In 2011, China launched Tiangong 1, and people began living on board in June 2012.

What is it for?

The International Space Station was built as a space-based research lab, where many experiments can be performed in zero gravity, like seeing how jumping spiders hunt when they are weightless (surprisingly well) or how fire burns (very strangely). To explore the Universe in the future, we have to learn how to survive for many years in the middle of space, and the ISS helps us carry out experiments so we can work out how to live in space for long periods of time by studying the effects of microgravity on the human body, animals and plants.

Earth can be seen from the many observation windows onboard.

Spiders can spin webs and jump very well in zero gravity.

The VEGGIE project, for example, has been created to allow astronauts to grow their own vegetables on board with nutrients and water – that'd be handy on a long trip! We also use the ISS to make observations of Earth, like monitoring coral reefs and climate change, and taking photos of hurricanes and volcanoes.

Fire burns as a circular flame in zero gravity.

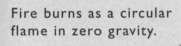

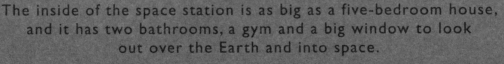

The inside of the space station is as big as a five-bedroom house, and it has two bathrooms, a gym and a big window to look out over the Earth and into space.

In the space station, crew members don't wear special clothes, like a space suit, but wear the same sort of clothes we wear on Earth. They don't have a washing machine, so astronauts will wear the same clothes for many days in a row. Most of the dirty clothing and other rubbish is sent back towards Earth, where it burns up in the atmosphere.

However, astronauts did have to wear special clothes on the space shuttle. These orange launch and entry jumpsuits were pumped full of air just like space suits, to protect the astronauts in case there was a problem with the spacecraft and it lost its air pressure.

SATELLITES

A satellite is simply an object that orbits the Earth. There are two kinds: natural satellites, like the Moon, and artificial satellites – the ones we've sent up into space. Since we invented rockets, people from many different countries have launched thousands of satellites into space, of all shapes and sizes. Some are like a small box and others as big as a lorry!

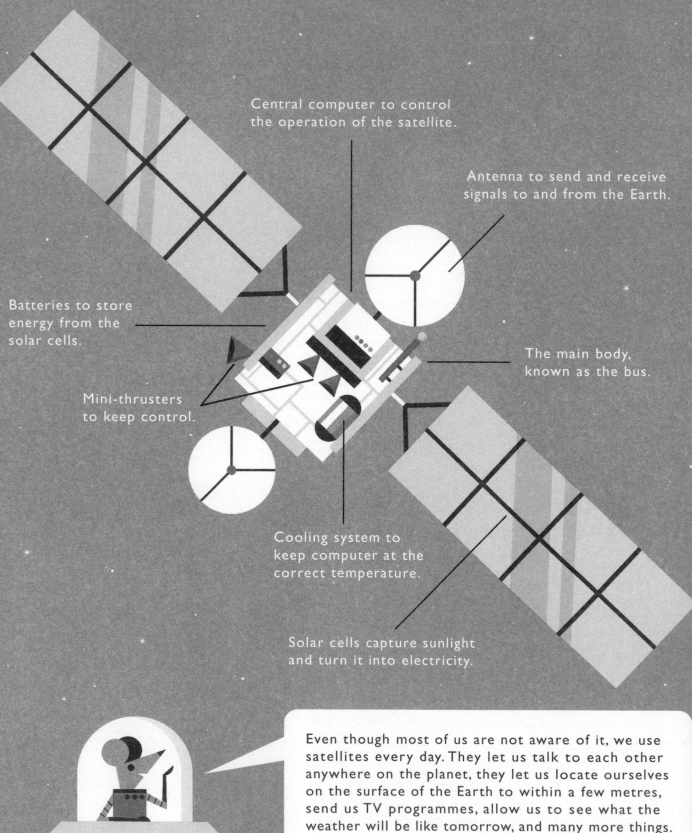

Central computer to control the operation of the satellite.

Antenna to send and receive signals to and from the Earth.

Batteries to store energy from the solar cells.

The main body, known as the bus.

Mini-thrusters to keep control.

Cooling system to keep computer at the correct temperature.

Solar cells capture sunlight and turn it into electricity.

Even though most of us are not aware of it, we use satellites every day. They let us talk to each other anywhere on the planet, they let us locate ourselves on the surface of the Earth to within a few metres, send us TV programmes, allow us to see what the weather will be like tomorrow, and many more things.

OBSERVATION SATELLITE

The first satellite to orbit the Earth was Sputnik, launched by the Soviets in 1957. It was a very simple spacecraft containing a battery, a thermometer and a radio transmitter.

SPUTNIK

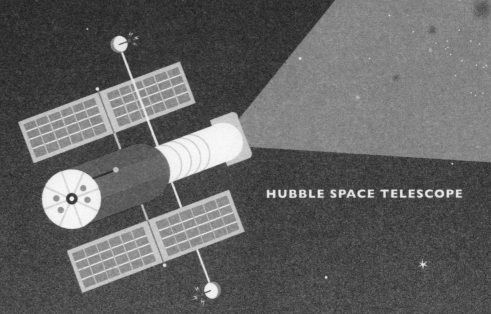

HUBBLE SPACE TELESCOPE

Science Satellites

The most famous of these is the Hubble space telescope, which has taken some of the best images of stars and galaxies. But there are many other space-based observatories looking at everything from the activity on the Sun through to the microwaves left over from the beginning of the Universe.

Weather and Earth Observation Satellites

Weather satellites look down at the Earth and observe what is happening in the atmosphere. They track clouds, measure wind speeds, look for rain and measure temperature all over the globe. This helps us predict our local weather, but also gathers data to monitor climate change. Earth observation satellites take photos of the surface of the Earth, and have been used to build maps and help us keep track of deforestation and the shrinking polar ice caps.

GPS

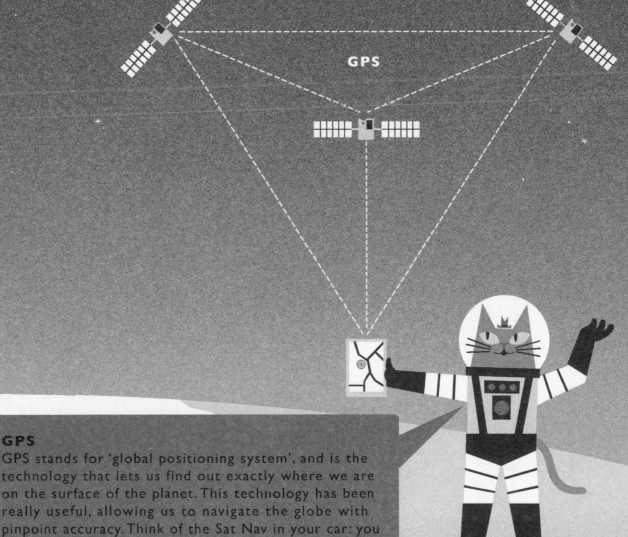

GPS

GPS stands for 'global positioning system', and is the technology that lets us find out exactly where we are on the surface of the planet. This technology has been really useful, allowing us to navigate the globe with pinpoint accuracy. Think of the Sat Nav in your car: you can travel anywhere in the world without getting lost.

MERCURY

Mercury is the closest planet to the Sun and the smallest planet in the solar system, only slightly larger than our Moon. Living so close to the awesome power of the Sun, the surface of Mercury is constantly battered with scorching rays, heating up to 350 degrees Celsius (662 degrees Fahrenheit). Meanwhile, the opposite side, facing the freezing cold of empty space, cools to -170 degrees Celsius (-274 degrees Fahrenheit). This means that one side is hot enough to melt metal and the other is twice as cold as the coldest place on Earth! Unlike Earth, Mercury has no atmosphere to reflect away the Sun's rays in the day and keep in the heat at night. This means that Mercury cannot keep its temperature stable, which is why it is a planet of two extremes.

Mercury is mostly made of heavy metals, which makes it a very dense planet. Imagine if this book was made of Mercury rock – it would be so heavy that you couldn't even pick it up! You would probably need a small crane to help you read it.

Having no atmosphere also means that Mercury has no protection against asteroids and comets hitting the surface. After billions of years of space rocks smashing into it, poor old Mercury has been left with a scarred and cratered surface.

MERCURY MESSENGER

Just like all of the other planets, no humans have ever visited Mercury. However, we are getting to know lots about the planet from a space probe we sent there called Messenger. Currently in orbit around the planet and packed with cameras and scientific instruments, Messenger has sent back thousands of images and other scientific data.

Mercury travels around the Sun in a very peculiar way, where a day on Mercury is longer than a year on Mercury! One day on Mercury is 176 Earth days, and one year on Mercury is 88 Earth days. If you were born on Mercury, you would be a lot older than you are on Earth. Grab a calculator to find out how old you would be if you lived there:

(your age) x 4.15 = your age on Mercury

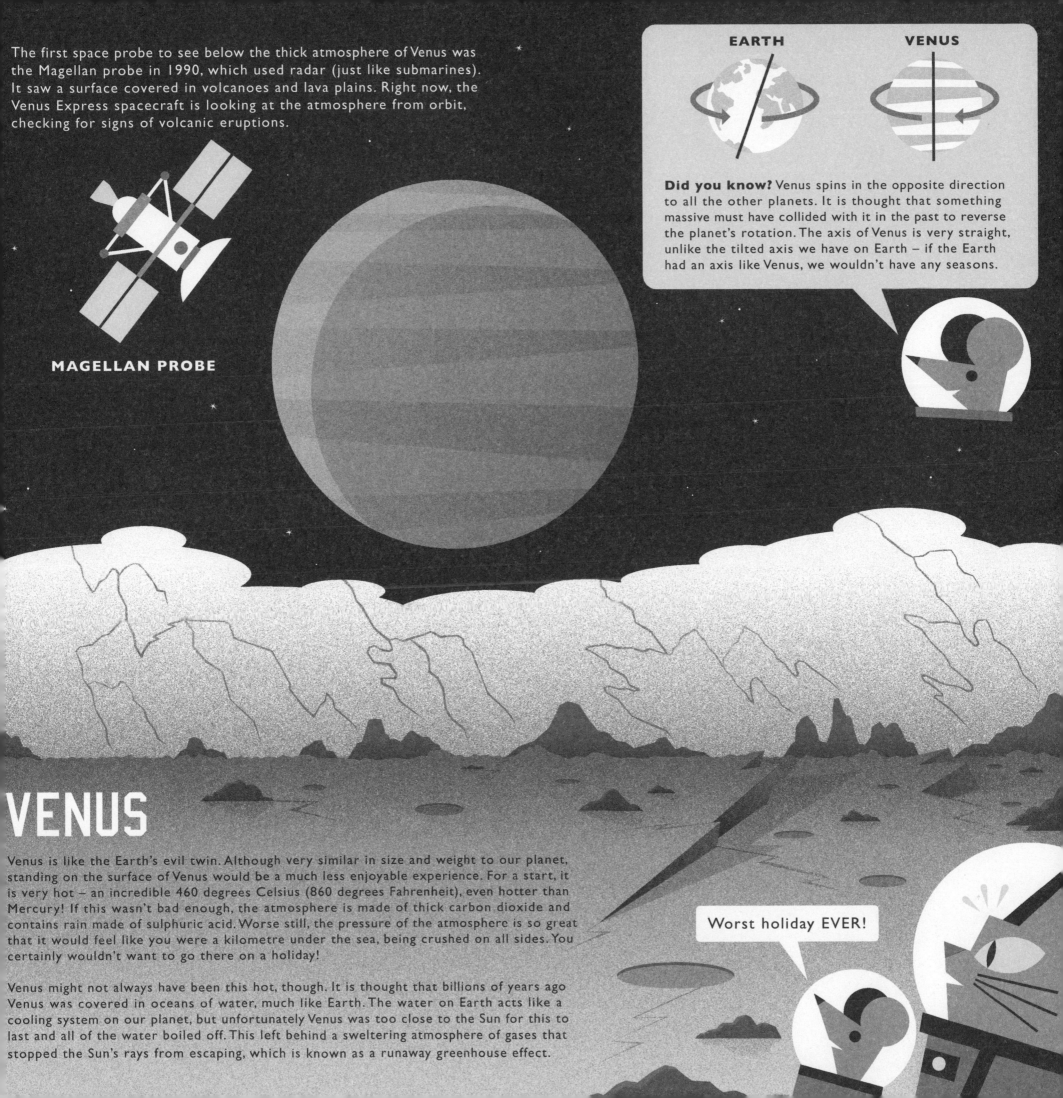

The first space probe to see below the thick atmosphere of Venus was the Magellan probe in 1990, which used radar (just like submarines). It saw a surface covered in volcanoes and lava plains. Right now, the Venus Express spacecraft is looking at the atmosphere from orbit, checking for signs of volcanic eruptions.

MAGELLAN PROBE

EARTH   VENUS

Did you know? Venus spins in the opposite direction to all the other planets. It is thought that something massive must have collided with it in the past to reverse the planet's rotation. The axis of Venus is very straight, unlike the tilted axis we have on Earth – if the Earth had an axis like Venus, we wouldn't have any seasons.

VENUS

Venus is like the Earth's evil twin. Although very similar in size and weight to our planet, standing on the surface of Venus would be a much less enjoyable experience. For a start, it is very hot – an incredible 460 degrees Celsius (860 degrees Fahrenheit), even hotter than Mercury! If this wasn't bad enough, the atmosphere is made of thick carbon dioxide and contains rain made of sulphuric acid. Worse still, the pressure of the atmosphere is so great that it would feel like you were a kilometre under the sea, being crushed on all sides. You certainly wouldn't want to go there on a holiday!

Venus might not always have been this hot, though. It is thought that billions of years ago Venus was covered in oceans of water, much like Earth. The water on Earth acts like a cooling system on our planet, but unfortunately Venus was too close to the Sun for this to last and all of the water boiled off. This left behind a sweltering atmosphere of gases that stopped the Sun's rays from escaping, which is known as a runaway greenhouse effect.

Worst holiday EVER!

MARS

Mars is a relatively small planet, about half as wide as the Earth. It has changed a lot since the birth of the solar system. In ancient history, Mars used to be warmer, with liquid water flowing across it and huge volcanoes bubbling away. We know this because we have seen flood channels on the surface, through which water once flowed, and occasionally flows today. It is possible that Mars once had large lakes and perhaps even an ocean. This has made scientists wonder if there used to be life on Mars, as liquid water is the key to life. Today, Mars is a dry and desolate planet, like a desert, with only a very thin atmosphere surrounding it. Because of its small size, over millions of years it slowly lost its internal heat to the cold of outer space, resulting in the water and lava freezing over.

MARS

DEIMOS

PHOBOS

Mars has two small moons, Phobos and Deimos. Phobos is about twice as wide as Deimos – about the width of a large city. Neither moon is a perfect circle; they are both knobbly and pimpled with crater marks. No one knows where the moons came from, but some scientists think they might be asteroids captured from space by Mars' gravity.

OLYMPUS MONS

Olympus Mons is a giant volcano on Mars that is about 25 kilometres/16 miles high, making it the tallest mountain in the solar system. It was built up from lava pouring out from the core over millions of years, although no lava flows there any more.

A year on Mars is about twice as long as a year on Earth. To work out your Mars age, just do this sum on a calculator:

(your age) x 0.5 = your age on Mars

Did you know? Mars' red colour comes from the iron oxide in the rocks. Iron oxide is also known as rust, which means the entire planet is rusting.

LIFE ON MARS?

We have sent many probes to Mars over the years. Successful past missions include the Opportunity and Spirit rovers, which drove around the Martian surface with many scientific instruments to take photos and sample the soil and wind. Opportunity was only meant to last 90 days, but it has now been in operation since 2004! On August 6th 2012, the NASA Curiosity rover touched down in the Gale Crater. Since landing on the surface of the planet, the car-sized rover has been crawling around the crater at a speed of 2 metres per minute. It is loaded with high-tech cameras and instruments that can zap Mars rocks with laser beams and gobble soil and rocks to see what they are made of. Why? To find out if Mars ever had the conditions to harbour life.

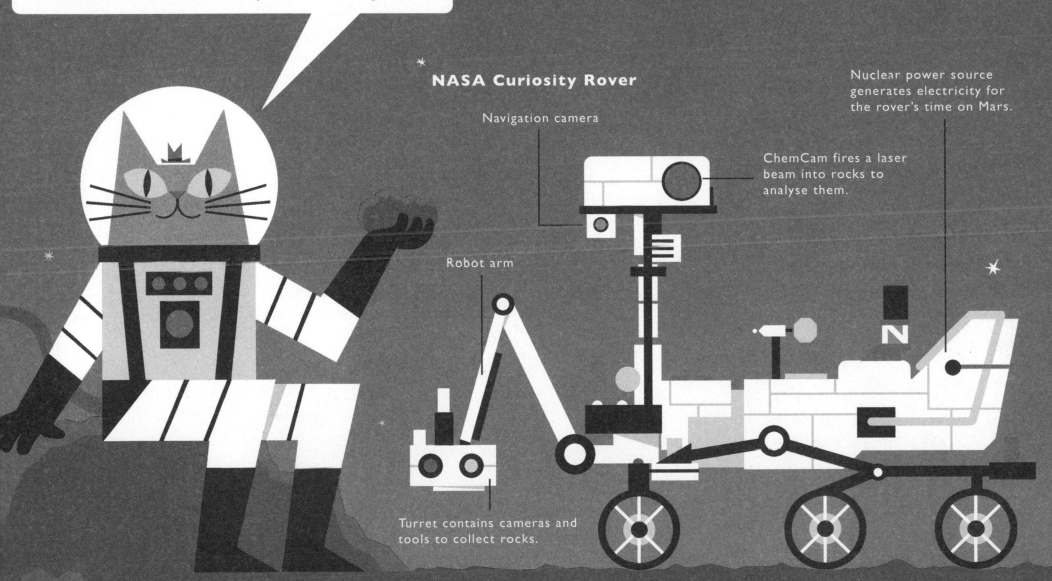

NASA Curiosity Rover

Navigation camera

Nuclear power source generates electricity for the rover's time on Mars.

ChemCam fires a laser beam into rocks to analyse them.

Robot arm

Turret contains cameras and tools to collect rocks.

Mars has a very thin atmosphere, with a few clouds thought to be made of water ice particles. It is believed that the atmosphere was ripped away from the planet by the Sun's solar wind because Mars has no magnetic field to protect it. Mars may have had a magnetic field once, but lost it when its liquid metal core cooled down and became solid.

JUPITER

Jupiter is a humongous ball of gas, so big that it could fit 1,300 Earths inside it. It is so massive that even if you added together all of the other planets, moons and asteroids in the solar system, they would make up less than half the mass of Jupiter. Jupiter is mostly made of hydrogen and helium, similar to the Sun – but unlike the Sun, Jupiter isn't on fire.

If you tried to land a spaceship on Jupiter, you would fall straight through the surface, because it is made of gas. Below this, the gas gradually turns into a vast liquid hydrogen ocean.

The atmosphere is constantly covered in violent boiling storms and has lightning, just like the lightning on our planet. The biggest of Jupiter's storms is the Great Red Spot, which is two or three times the size of Earth. It is a giant whirlwind that has been raging for hundreds of years, with wind speeds of up to 250 miles per hour.

Jupiter is so big that if aliens looked at our solar system they would probably only see the Sun and Jupiter and miss all of the rest! One day on Jupiter is only 10 hours long, which means it spins really fast for such a large planet! One year on Jupiter is around 12 Earth years.

Jupiter has over sixty moons and new ones are found every year. Four of them – Callisto, Europa, Ganymede and Io – are important, because they are very much like planets, with their own mixtures of ice, volcanoes and atmospheres. It's almost as if Jupiter has its own little solar system.

Callisto is a ball of rock and ice the size of Mercury. Scientists think it may have an ocean of salt water 100 kilometres under its surface that could possibly contain life.

Ganymede is the largest moon in the solar system, and the only one known to have its own liquid iron core, making it the only moon to have a large magnetic field.

Europa is very icy and is the smallest of Jupiter's four largest moons. The surface is crisscrossed with dark streaks and doesn't have many craters. This means that there is probably a huge ocean of liquid water under a surface of ice, cracking and straining under the tidal forces from Jupiter and the other moons. It is the most likely place in the solar system to have extraterrestrial life.

Io is a bright yellow moon, and is the most geologically active object in the solar system – the yellow colour is caused by frozen sulphur from the 400 active volcanoes on its surface. It travels really quickly around Jupiter, going all the way round in less than two Earth days.

It takes Jupiter nearly 12 Earth years to get around the Sun, which means that if you were born on Jupiter, you would only have one birthday every 12 years!

SATURN

Saturn is another gas giant similar to Jupiter, mostly made of hydrogen and helium, and is famous for the beautiful rings of ice encircling it. Even though Saturn is not as gigantic as Jupiter, it is still humongous, having more mass than all of the six smaller planets combined. Even though it is really big, Saturn is the least dense of all the planets and, rather surprisingly, it could float on water!

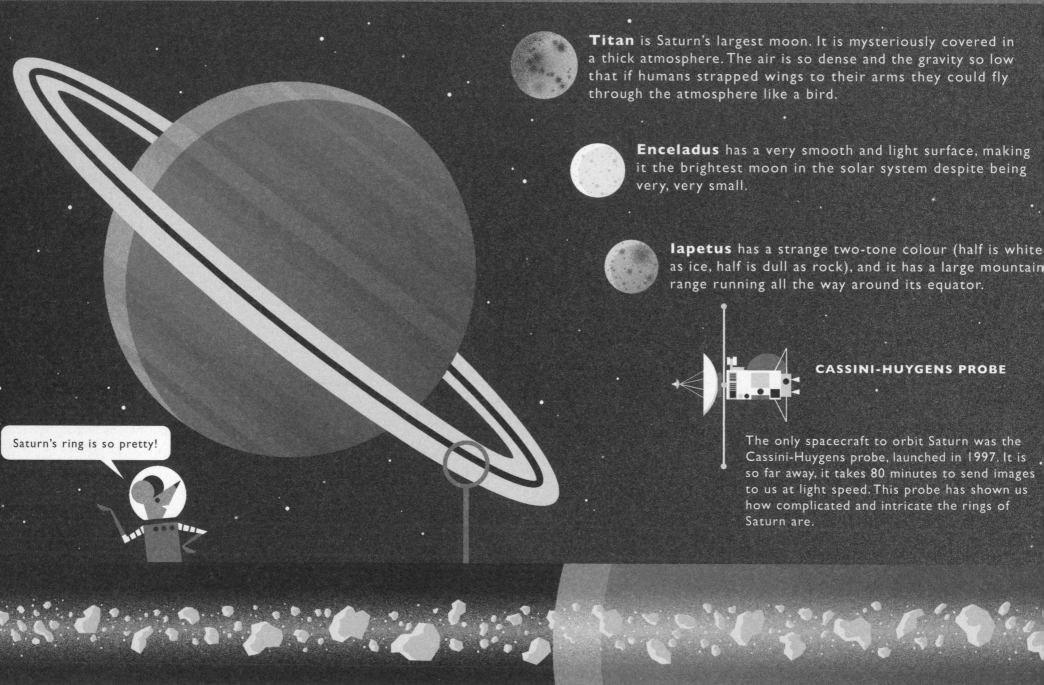

Titan is Saturn's largest moon. It is mysteriously covered in a thick atmosphere. The air is so dense and the gravity so low that if humans strapped wings to their arms they could fly through the atmosphere like a bird.

Enceladus has a very smooth and light surface, making it the brightest moon in the solar system despite being very, very small.

Iapetus has a strange two-tone colour (half is white as ice, half is dull as rock), and it has a large mountain range running all the way around its equator.

CASSINI-HUYGENS PROBE

The only spacecraft to orbit Saturn was the Cassini-Huygens probe, launched in 1997. It is so far away, it takes 80 minutes to send images to us at light speed. This probe has shown us how complicated and intricate the rings of Saturn are.

Saturn's ring is so pretty!

Why does Saturn have rings? Nobody knows for certain, but we know it is not alone. All the big gas giants – Jupiter, Uranus and Neptune – have their own rings, but the rings of Saturn are by far the biggest and most spectacular. The rings are made of tiny chunks of pure ice, which are mostly smaller than a centimetre but can be as big as a kilometre across. Astronomers don't know exactly how the rings formed, but think that they could either be from moons that got smashed up in the ancient past or material that never got to stick together because the gravity from Saturn and the other moons kept them apart.

URANUS

Uranus is another gas planet, just like Saturn and Jupiter, but unlike the other planets it spins on its side as if it has fallen over! No one knows exactly why it spins on its side, but it is likely to be due to a collision with a large object billions of years ago. Uranus also has rings, but they are far more difficult to see than those of Saturn, because they are made of dark bits of rock and dust.

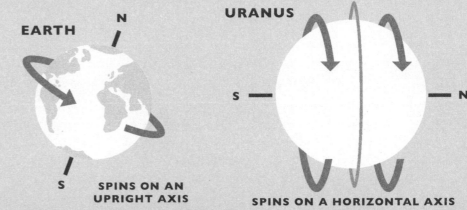

EARTH

N

S

SPINS ON AN UPRIGHT AXIS

URANUS

S — — N

SPINS ON A HORIZONTAL AXIS

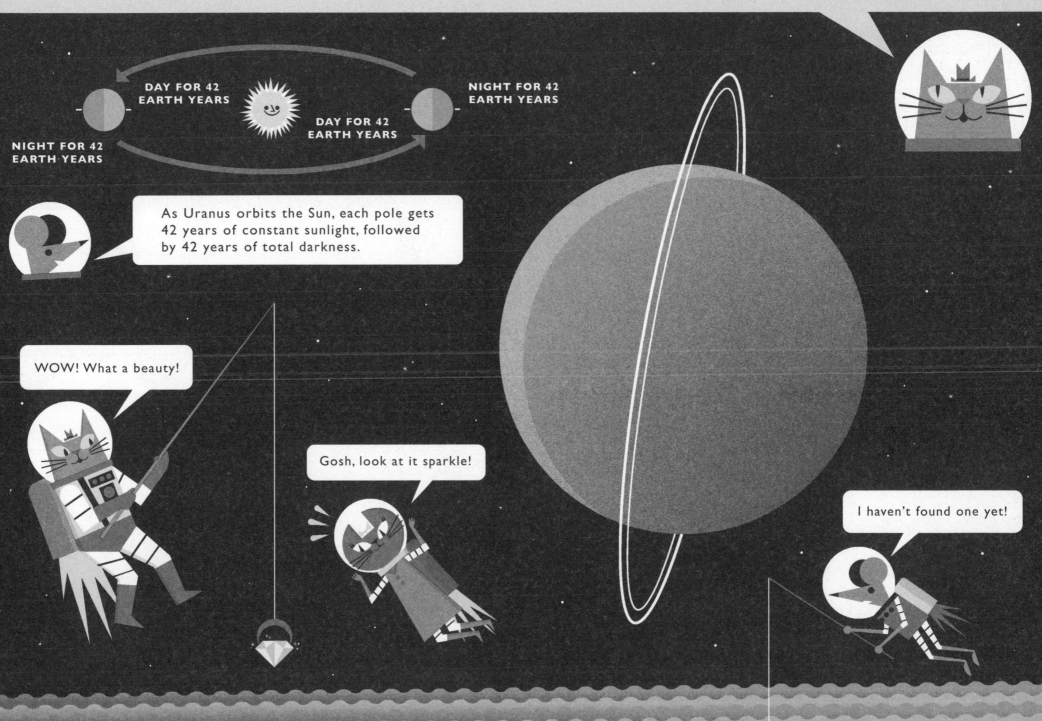

NIGHT FOR 42 EARTH YEARS

DAY FOR 42 EARTH YEARS

DAY FOR 42 EARTH YEARS

NIGHT FOR 42 EARTH YEARS

As Uranus orbits the Sun, each pole gets 42 years of constant sunlight, followed by 42 years of total darkness.

WOW! What a beauty!

Gosh, look at it sparkle!

I haven't found one yet!

The atmosphere of Uranus is the coldest in the solar system – as low as -224 degrees Celsius (-371.2 degrees Fahrenheit)! – but below this atmosphere lives a vast boiling ocean with temperatures high enough to melt metal. At the bottom of this ocean, between the carbon core and the liquid ocean above, scientists think there are trillions of diamonds floating about, created by the huge pressure and temperatures.

NEPTUNE

Neptune is named after the god of the sea because of its striking blue appearance. The furthest gas planet from the Sun and the last massive object before the depths of interstellar space, Neptune is another ice giant very similar to Uranus, but with a much more dramatic atmosphere. A day on Neptune is 16 hours long, and it takes 165 Earth years for Neptune to go around the Sun.

OUTER LAYER MADE FROM GASES

SMALL ROCKY CORE SAME SIZE AS EARTH

EARTH

NEPTUNE

At the centre of Neptune sits a rocky core, thought to be about the same size as the Earth. This core is super-hot, and as this energy boils up to the surface it makes the weather there really dramatic. The wind on the surface of Neptune is the fastest in the solar system, blowing as fast as a jet plane flies!

TRITON

Did you know?
It takes 165 Earth years for Neptune to travel around the Sun. So if you were born on Neptune, you would be ancient by the time you got to your first birthday!

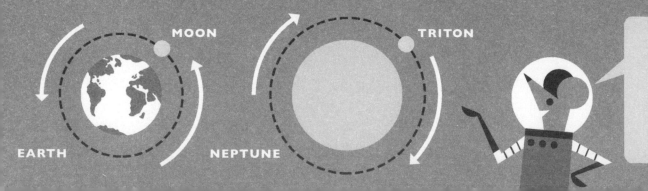

MOON

TRITON

EARTH

NEPTUNE

The largest of Neptune's moons, Triton, is very strange. It orbits the planet in the opposite direction to all the other large moons in the solar system, which means that it was probably captured by Neptune sometime in the past. Triton is slowly falling towards the surface of Neptune... and in the far future, it will be torn apart by Neptune's gravity.

ASTEROIDS AND COMETS

Apart from the planets and their moons, there are many other things flying about in our solar system, the most common being asteroids and comets. These chunks of rock and ice escaped being hoovered up by the planets in the early solar system and have been floating around ever since in the asteroid belt, Kuiper Belt and the Oort Cloud.

COMETS
Comets' tails always point in the opposite direction to the Sun.

SUN

Comets orbit the Sun differently to planets. In fact, they go nearer to the Sun than Mercury does!

ASTEROIDS

Asteroids

Asteroids come from the asteroid belt between Mars and Jupiter. The early solar system was a vast cloud of gas and dust which, over time, collected together into larger and larger chunks until they formed the planets and the moons. Asteroids are the chunks of rock that were left out of this planet-making party, and are mostly collected in the asteroid belt – asteroids anywhere else were hoovered up by the hungry planets as they grew. This is still going on today: every time you see a shooting star, it is an asteroid burning up as it flies through the Earth's atmosphere (although we call them meteors when they do this).

Comets

Comets come from the Kuiper Belt, beyond Neptune, or from far away in the Oort Cloud where icy rocks hang out. Occasionally, one of these rocks gets a slight nudge that sends it toppling in towards the centre of the solar system, like a big boulder rolling down a hill. As the comets approach the Sun, ice gets blasted off, leaving a huge icy tail trailing behind, which we can see from the Earth. These comets fly around the Sun and back out into the depth of space. Some only go around once, while others return like clockwork over and over again.

People are always on the lookout for asteroids or comets on a collision course with the Earth. Scientists are almost certain that a large asteroid impact killed off the dinosaurs, and we don't want the same thing to happen to us! Fortunately, most meteors are very small and just burn up in the atmosphere, never reaching the ground.

THE NIGHT SKY

Northern Hemisphere **Winter**

On a clear night, these star maps help show you the layout of the stars in the different seasons. All you need is a compass to find out which way north is, then lie on your back with your head pointing north and your feet pointing south. The western horizon will be to your right and the eastern horizon will be to your left. This is the opposite of how we normally see east and west, which is based on looking down at the ground – but don't worry, these maps are not wrong! The maps should now line up with the stars above your head and you can start constellation hunting.

What are constellations? Constellations are groups of stars in the sky that people in ancient times joined together into pictures – just like a dot-to-dot drawing. Grouping the stars together like this helps us track them as they slide over the sky in the different months of the year.

Orion is known as the Hunter. Gemini are twins standing next to each other. Ursa Major is known as the Great Bear, or the Big Dipper. Ursa Minor is known as the Little Bear. Cassiopeia is a big W shape, and is easy to see even in the city. The Andromeda galaxy is the only spiral galaxy outside our own that we can see with the naked eye.

THE NIGHT SKY
Northern Hemisphere **Spring**

N

NE

NW

Lacerta

Cassiopeia

Cygnus

Cepheus

Perseus

Lyra

Camelopardalis

Draco

Ursa Minor

Aquila

Hercules

Corona Borealis

Lynx

Orion

E

W

Serpens Caput

Bootes

Ursa Major

Gemini

Canes Venatici

MARS

Cancer

Leo

Monoceros

SATURN

Virgo

Hydra

Sextans

SE

SW

Corvus

Crater

S

As the Earth travels around the Sun, we see different parts of the Universe in our night sky. That's why we need a different star map for each season.

THE NIGHT SKY

Northern Hemisphere **Summer**

The best time to look at the stars is on a clear night with no clouds. It's also good to get out into the countryside, because the lights of the city make it difficult to see anything but the brightest stars. Find a comfortable place to look at the sky, and watch more and more stars appear as your eyes get used to the dark.

N

NE

NW

Perseus

Auriga

Lynx

Camelopardalis

Andromeda

Cassiopeia

Ursa Minor

Ursa Major

VENUS

Pegasus

Cepheus

Leo Minor

Lacerta

Draco

MARS

E

Canes Venatici

W

Cygnus

Boötes

SATURN

Delphinus

Lyra

Corona Borealis

Hercules

Equuleus

Virgo

Aquila

Serpens Caput

Ophiuchus

SE

Libra

SW

S

If you are really lucky, you might see a shooting star: a blaze of light streaking across the sky as a meteor burns up in the Earth's atmosphere. These are quite rare and only last for a fraction of a second, so they're a real challenge to spot. They happen all year round, but August or November are the best times to see them, because this is when the Earth flies through patches of space dust.

The planets of our solar system roam around against the backdrop of the constellations. They can easily be mistaken for stars, but there are a few subtle differences that can help us to spot them. The planets shine with a more stable light than the stars, which tend to twinkle. Also, the planets move across our sky from one day to the next, and so are never in the same place. The planets always hang around near the horizon.

THE NIGHT SKY
Northern Hemisphere **Autumn**

N

NE

NW

Ursa Major

Lynx

Boötes

Auriga

Ursa Minor

Camelopardalis

Corona Borealis

Draco

Cepheus

Perseus

Cassiopeia

Cygnus

Hercules

Taurus

Lyra

E

W

Andromeda

Lacerta

Aries

Aquila

Delphinus

Pegasus

Pisces

Equuleus

Cetus

**URANUS
JUPITER**

Aquarius

SE

NEPTUNE

SW

S

Jupiter and Venus are the easiest planets to spot, shining brighter than any other star with brilliant white light. Mars is the next easy to spot, because it shines with an orange colour, unlike the other stars and planets. Mercury, Saturn and Uranus are more difficult to see, but are still visible to the naked eye. But to see Neptune, you'll need to use a telescope!

TELESCOPES

Just about everything we know about space comes from what we discovered through the lenses of telescopes. We have used them for centuries to discover the planets, moons, stars and galaxies. By looking at the tiny movements of all of these objects in the sky, we have been able to work out a huge amount more about the Universe – like the mass of the galaxy, the speed of light and the amount of matter the Universe contains.

Radio

Radio telescopes are large ground-based dishes. The biggest are built into natural craters in the mountains.

Incoming radio waves

Incoming radio waves

Radio waves reflect off the dish

Receiver amplifies and detects radio signals

They are also built into long lines of smaller dishes that, when added all together, act like one huge dish.

These telescopes do not really 'see' space, like the optical telescopes. Instead, they tune into radio waves coming from space and then draw them out on graphs for scientists to look at. Radio telescopes allow us to see the most exotic objects in the Universe, like black holes, pulsars, quasars and even the origins of the Universe itself.

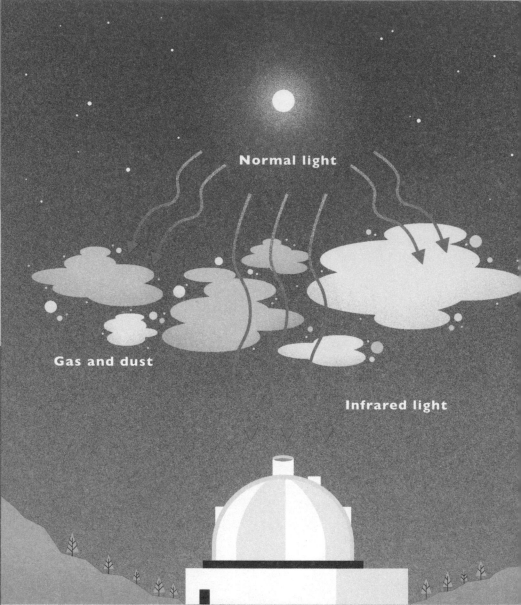

Normal light

Gas and dust

Infrared light

Infrared

Infrared telescopes look at anything in the Universe that gives off heat, and are used to see objects that don't give off visible light or are hidden behind gas and dust (normal light gets absorbed by gas and dust, but infrared light goes straight through). There have been infrared telescopes on the ground and in space, and even on the back of an airplane!

Radio Waves   **Micro Waves**   **Infrared**

Many telescopes look at light, just like we do with our eyes. However, this is not the only thing we can use telescopes to look at. Beyond the colours of the rainbow – before red and after violet – lies a realm of other colours that our eyes can't see; these all form part of what is known as the electromagnetic spectrum.

We can, however, build telescopes that look at these other kinds of light, and we have learned a huge amount of information about the Universe by doing this. Below is a picture of all of the different kinds of light in the electromagnetic spectrum and the telescopes that have looked at them.

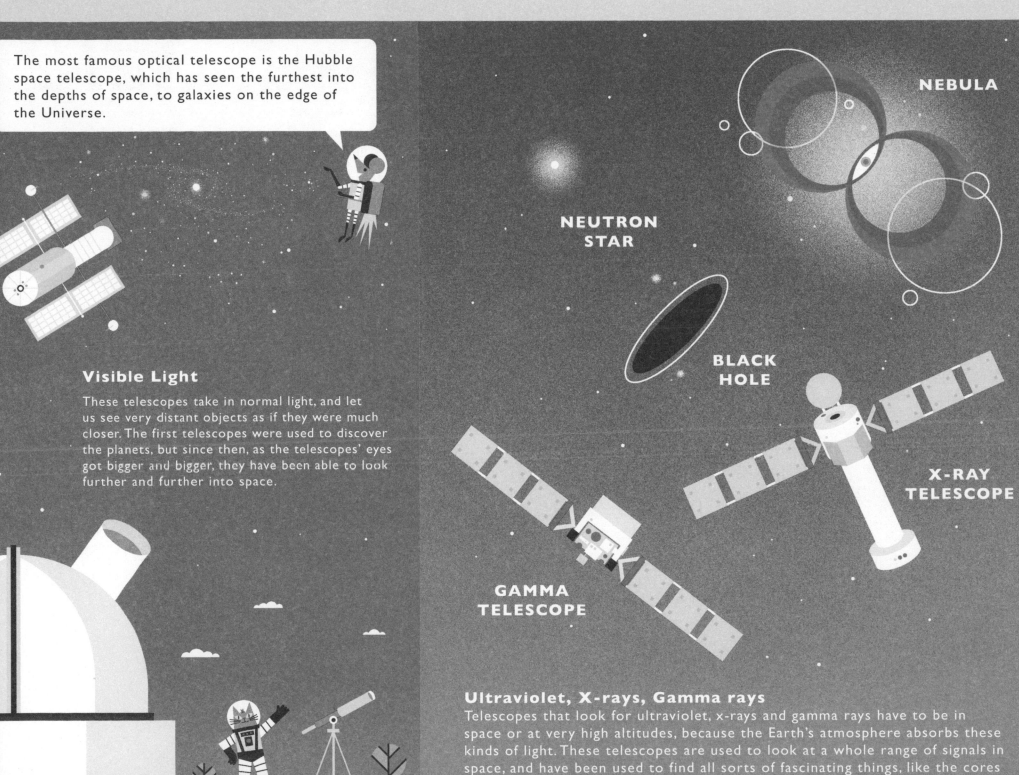

The most famous optical telescope is the Hubble space telescope, which has seen the furthest into the depths of space, to galaxies on the edge of the Universe.

NEBULA

NEUTRON STAR

BLACK HOLE

X-RAY TELESCOPE

GAMMA TELESCOPE

Visible Light

These telescopes take in normal light, and let us see very distant objects as if they were much closer. The first telescopes were used to discover the planets, but since then, as the telescopes' eyes got bigger and bigger, they have been able to look further and further into space.

Ultraviolet, X-rays, Gamma rays

Telescopes that look for ultraviolet, x-rays and gamma rays have to be in space or at very high altitudes, because the Earth's atmosphere absorbs these kinds of light. These telescopes are used to look at a whole range of signals in space, and have been used to find all sorts of fascinating things, like the cores of galaxies, nebulae, supernovae, neutron stars and black holes.

Visible Light   **Ultraviolet**   **X-Rays**   **Gamma Rays**

THE DEATH OF STARS

The stars in the night sky don't last forever. Eventually, the fuel they burn runs out and they end their lives in a huge explosion. When a star runs out of hydrogen, it starts to fuse heavier and heavier elements together, which are then blown out into space when the star explodes. These elements make up all of the stuff around us: the Earth, the plants and animals, even ourselves – so the death of a star is not only an ending but also the beginning of something new.

In billions of years, when the Sun finally uses up all its fuel, it will expand into a big red giant and then collapse under its own weight into a white dwarf. This hot, dense body, the size of the Earth, will no longer fuse atoms together, and will slowly cool down as it loses its heat to space.

At many times the mass of our Sun, the supergiant stars burn off their fuel much quicker and end their lives in spectacular fashion, with a humongous explosion called a supernova. In a few hours, a supernova releases more energy than our Sun will in its entire lifetime and shines as brightly as an entire galaxy! This supernova explosion leaves behind a giant cloud of debris, which is called a nebula.

YELLOW STAR

THE STAR GRADUALLY GROWS BIGGER AND BIGGER ONCE IT HAS USED UP ALL OF ITS FUEL

THE STAR BECOMES SO BIG, IT COLLAPSES UNDER ITS OWN WEIGHT AND EXPLODES INTO A SMALL WHITE DWARF STAR

RED GIANT STAR

WHITE DWARF STAR

SUPERGIANT STAR

THE SUPERGIANT STAR EXPLODES IN A SUPERNOVA

SUPERNOVA

NEUTRON STAR

After the supernova explosion, the core of the star collapses into a super-dense body known as a neutron star. It is so dense that a mere sugar cube-sized piece of a neutron star would weigh as much as Mount Everest!

The biggest explosions in the Universe come from the biggest stars: the hypergiants! At more than a thousand times the mass of the Sun, they blow up in an even bigger explosion called a hypernova. The core of a hypergiant collapses so hard and fast that it rips a hole in space and time, creating a black hole. A black hole has such strong gravity that not even light can escape!

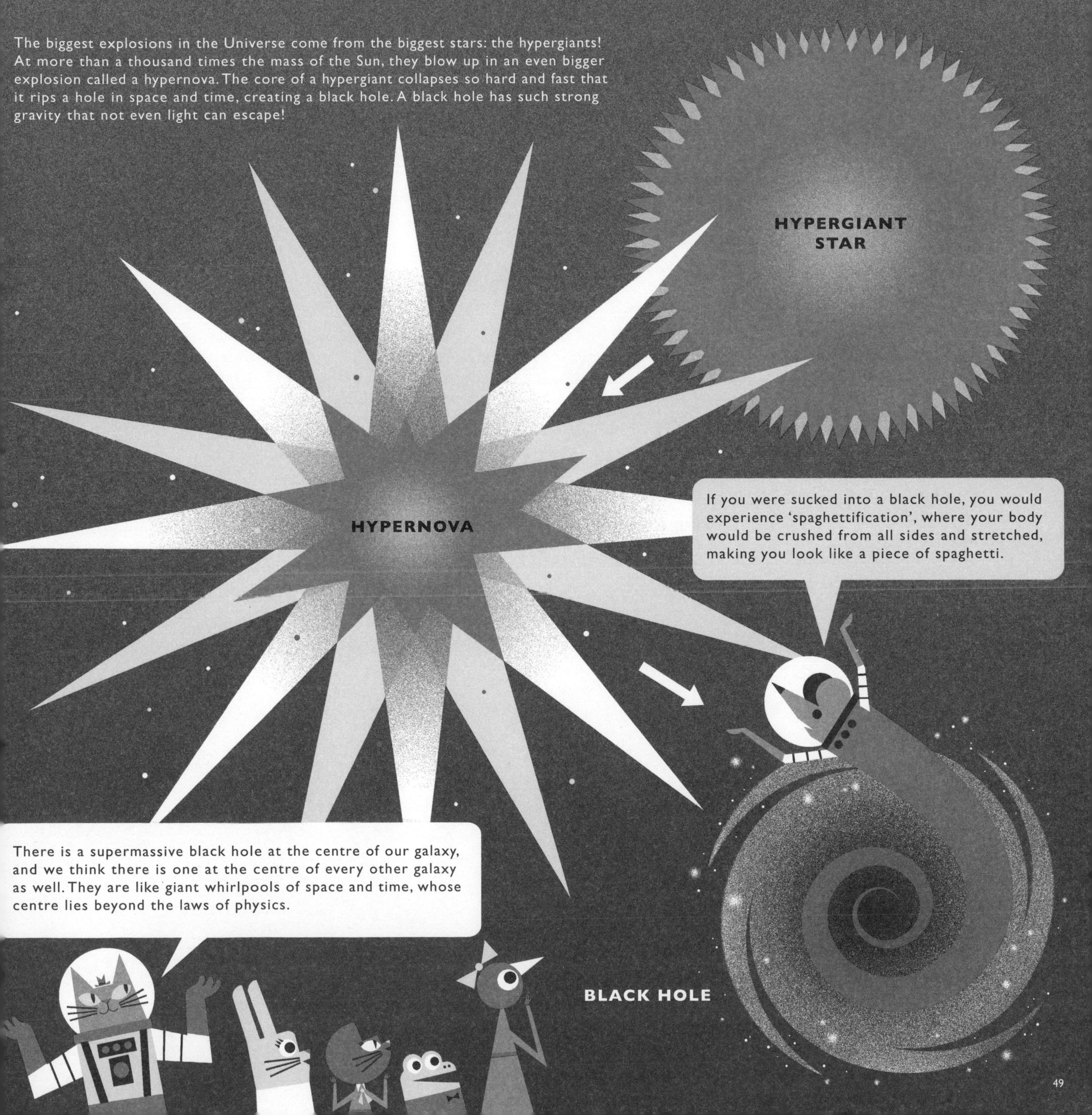

HYPERGIANT STAR

HYPERNOVA

If you were sucked into a black hole, you would experience 'spaghettification', where your body would be crushed from all sides and stretched, making you look like a piece of spaghetti.

There is a supermassive black hole at the centre of our galaxy, and we think there is one at the centre of every other galaxy as well. They are like giant whirlpools of space and time, whose centre lies beyond the laws of physics.

BLACK HOLE

LIFE IN THE UNKNOWN

We live on a planet orbiting a star, and when we look out into space we can see many, many other stars. So a logical question is: are there other beings out there, living on other planets orbiting other stars?

So far, we don't know for certain if there is life anywhere else in the Universe, but the more we learn about life on Earth, and about space, the more likely it seems that we are not the only planet with plants and animals. Maybe there are even planets with intelligent life on them like us!

Some clues about where life in space might live comes from microbes on Earth that thrive in extreme conditions, like at the bottom of the ocean, where there is no light, or in poisonous lakes. If life can exist there, then it might also exist below the ice caps of Jupiter's moon Europa, or in strange chemical pools on other planets.

On Earth, rich bundles of life exist around vents deep under the sea. Because these ecosystems are completely dark, they might also exist on faraway moons in the solar system, so long as there is liquid water and a rich chemical soup.

Sludge eels could be hoovering up microscopic animals that float around hydrothermal vents.

Scientists think that one in five stars have a planet like the Earth in close orbit. This means that there could be tens of billions of planets in our galaxy with life on them. Scientists have discovered many hundreds of planets flying around other stars out in the galaxy, and they keep finding more. A space telescope called the Kepler Probe is constantly on the lookout for new Earth-like planets, and there is a good chance that one day we'll find one just like the Earth.

Finding another planet with any kind of microbes on it would be amazing, but it would be even more incredible to find a planet with intelligent life on it! Finding another civilisation in the skies would be the most amazing discovery in history, because it would mean that we are not alone in the Universe. So far, we haven't found any signals from outer space that give a sign of intelligent life, although the search continues.

Maybe there are spindle squids that are the top predators, hunting and eating other animals living around the hydrothermal vents.

LIFE IN THE UNKNOWN

So if we did find aliens, what would they be like?

All life on Earth is made up of carbon atoms, but this might not be the only equation for life. Silicon is a similar kind of atom to carbon, and so life on other planets could be made of silicon atoms instead. Silicon is what sand on the beach is made of, and is also what we use to make computer chips.

There are bacteria on Earth called snottites (because they look like snot!) that can exist in extreme acid conditions, so some planets could have sulfur-based beasts, who are immune to sulfuric acid.

Most life needs oxygen to breathe, but we have worms on Earth that breathe methane, the main ingredient of bottom burps. Saturn's moon Titan is covered in methane, so it might have some other type of farty aliens swimming about in its methane sea.

The water bear is a little creature from Earth that can survive in outer space without a space suit! Perhaps there are creatures out there that don't need a spaceship to travel to other planets – they just glide there on giant solar wings.

On a big, dense, rocky planet, the force of gravity would be much bigger, which would mean that the aliens would have to be a lot stronger just to support their own weight. Also, everything would be much smaller, because anything big would break.

At the opposite end of the scale, planets with a much lower gravity would allow for plants and animals to grow much bigger, because everything would be so light. Combined with a dense oxygen atmosphere, the sky would be like the ocean on Earth, and you could get giant alien sky whales swimming through the air.

FUTURE OF SPACE

What is the future of space travel?

In the past, the only way of getting into space was by joining one of the space agencies and going on scientific missions. However, in the future anyone will be able to go into space by buying a ticket for a seat on a spaceship, just like how we fly in airplanes now. It will be really expensive to begin with, but it will become more affordable over time.

If you do join a space agency and become an astronaut, you might get to be part of a new raft of exciting missions. You might be part of a team building a base on the Moon. In the moonbase, you would mine the Moon for rare elements and materials to build spaceships with. You might also go on a long mission to Mars, to explore the surface and try to find out if anything else ever lived there.

Almost there, folks!

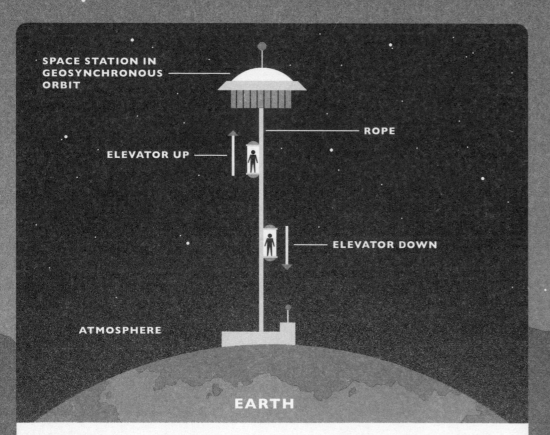

SPACE STATION IN GEOSYNCHRONOUS ORBIT

ROPE

ELEVATOR UP

ELEVATOR DOWN

ATMOSPHERE

EARTH

Another idea to get people into space would be to build a space elevator. This would be like a really long rope going out into space that would always hover over the same point on the Earth. Although very difficult to build, it would be a much cheaper way to get things to and from space than having to launch rockets all the time.

In future, space suits might be made of skintight material rather than being pressurised. They would just have a pressurised helmet to let us breathe. These suits would be much more manoeuvrable, but much more difficult to put on.

Oh, it's very snug.

People might start taking holidays in giant space stations built on the surface of other planets or moons. The space cities would be made out of materials mined from the planet, and would be protected from the vacuum of space with big domes full of air for people to breathe. A giant space city would capture energy from the Sun with huge solar panels, and people would grow plants to eat in giant greenhouses. Instead of airports, there would be spaceports, allowing people to fly from one planet to another.

FUTURE OF SPACE

The kind of spaceships we have now will never be able to travel faster than the speed of light. However, when they start travelling really, really fast in future, a rather peculiar thing will happen. The quicker they travel through space, the slower they will travel through time! This is an effect of relativity – a principle of physics discovered by Albert Einstein. If someone outside the spaceship looked at the people inside, it would look as though they were moving in really slow motion. But to the people inside the spaceship, everything would move at a normal speed, but the journey to their destination would be a lot shorter. This means that a voyage of a thousand years would feel like only ten minutes! This would be one way to travel really far around the galaxy, although it would take a huge amount of energy.

To get to other stars and planets, the people might be put into a deep
sleep called 'suspended animation' for hundreds of years. Robots would
fly the spaceships all the way and wake the people up when they arrived.

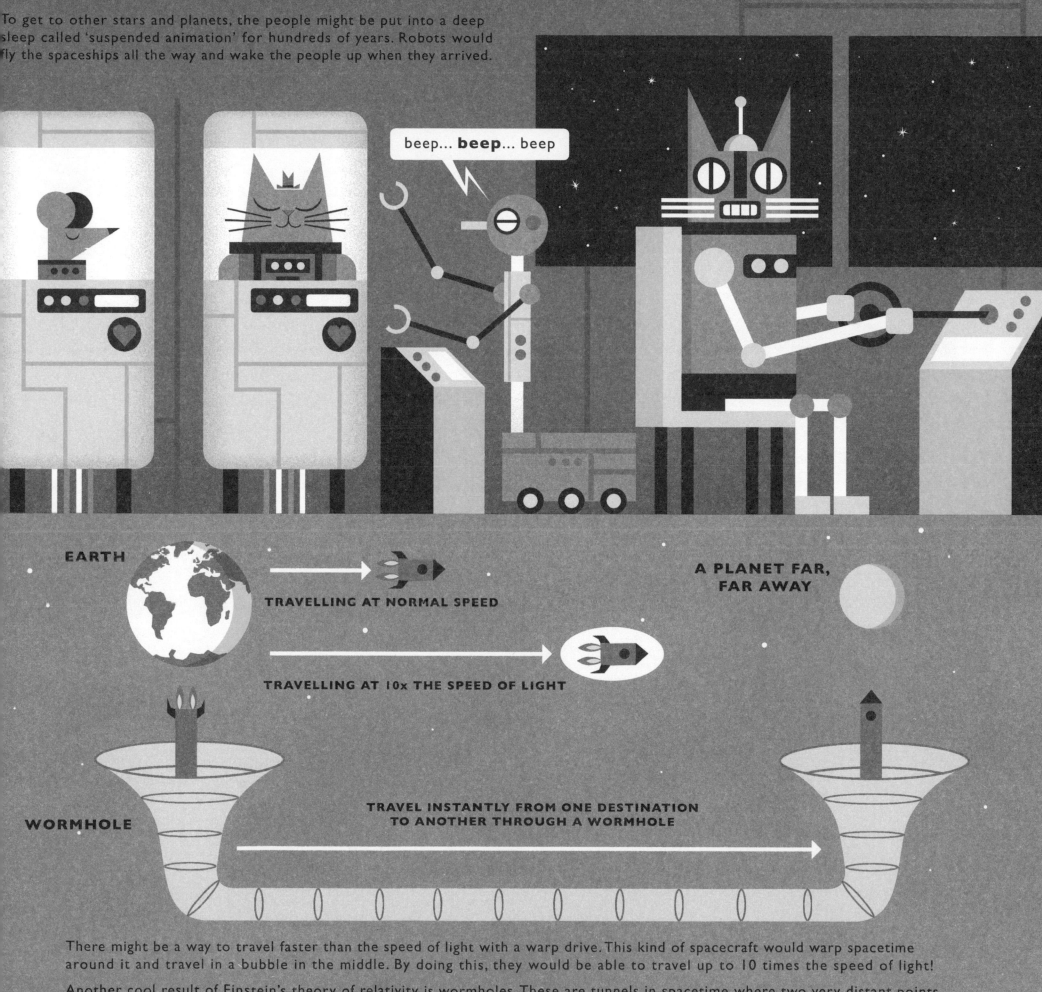

beep... **beep**... beep

EARTH

TRAVELLING AT NORMAL SPEED

TRAVELLING AT 10x THE SPEED OF LIGHT

A PLANET FAR,
FAR AWAY

WORMHOLE

TRAVEL INSTANTLY FROM ONE DESTINATION
TO ANOTHER THROUGH A WORMHOLE

There might be a way to travel faster than the speed of light with a warp drive. This kind of spacecraft would warp spacetime
around it and travel in a bubble in the middle. By doing this, they would be able to travel up to 10 times the speed of light!

Another cool result of Einstein's theory of relativity is wormholes. These are tunnels in spacetime where two very distant points
in normal space are connected to each other. If they exist, it would mean that you could travel from one part of the Universe to
another in an instant!

To travel to another planet or moon in the solar system, you don't travel in a straight line towards it, because it would always be moving. You have to work out where it'll be in the future and aim there! It takes lots of clever people and computers to work this out.

The word 'galaxy' comes from the Greek 'galaxias' meaning 'milky circle', which is also how our Milky Way galaxy got its name.

In the past, people thought that the Earth was the centre of the solar system. A man called Nicolaus Copernicus was the first person to say that the Sun was at the centre, with the Earth flying around it.

The first rockets were made 1,000 years ago in China.

There are still many mysteries out there waiting to be solved in the great depths of space, and with each discovery will come just as many new questions. So now, my friends, this curious cat has to shoot off and see what he can find! I could always do with some help from brave astronauts and scientists – so keep your eyes on our skies and, who knows, perhaps one day you'll venture into the stars in your own spaceship and help solve the mysteries at the Frontiers of Space!

GLOSSARY

Asteroid
A rock orbiting the Sun, mainly closer to the Sun than Jupiter.

Astronaut/Cosmonaut
A person trained by a space agency who flies in space.

Atom
The basic building block of matter, made of protons, neutrons and electrons. There are many different kinds of atoms called elements (like hydrogen, helium and oxygen, for example).

Black Hole
A hole in space and time that sucks in matter and light.

Comet
An icy rock that has a tail when flying close to the Sun.

Density
A measurement of how much mass there is in a certain space.

Electromagnetic Spectrum
The name for all of the different kinds of light. It contains radio waves, infrared radiation, visible light, ultraviolet light, x-rays and gamma rays.

ESA
The European Space Agency.

Fusion Reaction
When two atoms are crushed together to make a new atom, which releases lots of energy.

Galaxy
A collection of billions of stars.

Gas
A loose collection of high-energy atoms.

Gravity
An invisible force that pulls matter together.

Helium
The second most common element in the Universe, also burned in the middle of the Sun.

Hubble Space Telescope
A telescope that orbits the Earth and takes amazing pictures of distant objects in space.

Hydrogen
The most common element in the Universe, made of a proton and an electron. This is what the Sun burns.

Hypergiant
A loose term used to describe the biggest and brightest stars in the Universe.

International Space Station
Orbiting the Earth, it was built by many countries around the world working together.

Mass
A measure of the amount of matter something is made of.

Matter
The stuff that planets, stars and people are made of – large collections of atoms all stuck together.

Meteorite
A meteoroid big enough to reach the ground without burning up completely.

Meteoroid
A piece of space rock that flies into the Earth's atmosphere and burns up.

Molecule
A group of atoms stuck together.

NASA
The United States of America's space agency, which has made many space missions, including landing people on the Moon.

Nebula
The gases and debris left over by a supernova.

Neutron Star
An incredibly dense star left over by a supernova explosion.

Oxygen
The third most common element in the Universe, and what we humans need to breathe.

Planet
A large body that orbits a star and has cleared its orbit of other objects.

Planetoid
Any kind of body that orbits the Sun.

Pulsars
Fast-spinning neutron stars that beam out radio waves.

Quasars
A supermassive black hole in the centre of a distant galaxy giving off huge amounts of light.

Solar Panel
Collects sunlight and turns it into electricity.

Solar System
A group of planets, moons, asteroids and comets, and the star that they orbit.

Space Shuttle
A reusable spacecraft built by NASA.

Speed of Light
A measurement of how fast light travels through empty space.

Supergiant
A very big star, with a mass more than 10 times that of our Sun.

Supermassive Black Hole
A massive black hole thought to be found at the centre of every galaxy.

Supernova
The explosion at the end of a supergiant star.

Temperature
A measurement of how hot or cold something is.

Weightlessness
The feeling you have in space when there is no gravity holding you down and where you float in mid-air.

X-Rays
A type of high-energy light given off by stars and other high-energy objects.

Outer space is very complicated. Use this glossary to help you understand and remember some of the amazing things in this book.

The authors would like to thank:

BEN NEWMAN

Dedicated to Kathy, Claire and Colin Newman.

Special thank you to Bjorn Lie, Tom Frost, George Mellor, Jim Stoten, Owen Gildersleeve, Felt Mistress, Lauren Braithwaite, James Wilson, the Nobrow team and of course, Dominic Walliman and Alex Spiro.

DOMINIC WALLIMAN

For Megan and Isabelle.

Special thank you to Nicholas and Ursula Walliman, Ben Walliman, Claudia Walliman Gomez, Tessa and Phil Taylor, and all the people at Flying Eye Books, Alex Spiro, and especially Ben Newman.

RECOMMENDED READING

Big Book of Stars & Planets – Emily Bone and Fabiano Fiorin
National Geographic Little Kids First Big Book of Space – Catherine D. Hughes and David A. Aguilar
Space A Children's Encyclopedia – DK

Every attempt has been made to ensure that any statements written as fact have been checked to the best of our abilities. However, we are still human, thankfully, and occasionally little mistakes may crop up. Should this happen, please email info@nobrow.net with any erroneous passages and we will be sure to amend the text accordingly for future editions of this book.

This is an eighth edition. First published in 2013.

Published by Flying Eye Books, an imprint of Nobrow Ltd. 27 Westgate Street, London, E8 3RL.

ISBN 978-1-909263-07-9
Printed in Poland on FSC® certified paper.

Order from www.flyingeyebooks.com

FSC
www.fsc.org
MIX
Paper from
responsible sources
FSC® C118475

Order from flyingeyebooks.com

978-1-909263-60-4

Switch your brain to stun and hold on tight because Professor Astro Cat is ready to take you on a journey through the incredible world of physics. Learn about energy, forces and the building blocks of you, me and the universe in this mind-blowing **ATOMIC ADVENTURE**!

Find us and Professor Astro Cat on twitter
@FlyingEyeBooks   @ProfAstroCat

Download the app now!

**Professor Astro Cat's
Solar System**

"Professor Astro Cat's Solar System is the educational app kids will actually want."

— The Huffington Post

www.minilabstudios.com